THE FIRST TEN YEARS IN AUSTRALIA

THE FIRST TEN YEARS IN AUSTRALIA

By a Ten Year Old Ten Pound Pom

MAX BARRINGTON

Etteleah

CONTENTS

1	1
2	2
3	3
4	4
5	5
6	11
7	25
8	33
9	38
10	47
11	55
12	71
13	88

CHAPTER 1

The First Ten Years In Australia
From a Ten Year old, Ten Pound Pom in 1959
Max Barrington
This book is based on a true story, names, dates and places may have been changed.

CHAPTER 2

Other Books By Max Barrington
Woolgar River Curse:
Receiving a phone call announcing that you are the heir to a 70,000 acre cattle property that is complete with a five bedroom mansion would be like winning the Lotto.
But to Gus and Lynette Teague, it was the beginning of a discovery into corruption, deceit, tragedy and murder.
Was it really an 'Aboriginal Curse' on that property that caused the death of a family of five, or simply tragic events?
Task:
I was looking to make a few dollars until my next work project started. "Check out the Air Tasking pages on Facebook," they said.
An Australian road trip from Cairns to Darwin turns into Mystery, Intrigue and Life Threatening Danger
Dying to Find Gold:
Fossicking for Gold in Australia is a popular activity
But when Mick West's, best mate goes missing whilst on a fossicking trip
The police suspect Mick of murder
Harry Croft:
When Harry's beloved wife is taken from him by reckless youths in a stolen car, he decides to reinstate justice the way it was when he was a police sergeant many years before

CHAPTER 3

The First Ten Years In Australia
From a Ten Year old, Ten Pound Pom in 1959
Max Barrington

This story follows ***ten*** years of a boy's life, who, at the age of ***ten***, in the year 1959, was brought to Australia from England by his parents, who participated in the Assisted Passage Migration Scheme, which was created in 1945 by the 'Chifley Government' and its first Minister for Immigration, Arthur Calwell.

The scheme was intended to substantially increase the population of Australia and to supply workers for the country's booming industries.

This story, tells of a family's uncertain migration to a new life in a country that they had only read about in brochures issued by the Australian Government.

It tells of the many hardships and good times, the family experienced in the transition period of that time.

It tells of the ***ten*** moves the family made to different New South Wales towns within the first ***ten*** years.

It will take you back to how things were in Australia, in the 1960's

It is such an adventure, that, you may not be able to put this book down.

Although this book is based on a true story, some names, circumstances, places, locations and events have been fictionalised to avoid recognition.

CHAPTER 4

*For the love of my life,
my darling wife and my inspiration,
Lynette*

CHAPTER 5

The Journey

They had arrived in London by train from Blackpool, a journey of two hundred and forty miles, the longest journey Peter had ever been on, in his ten years since birth.

The family had stayed in London for three days with Peter's uncle Gordon, who had a residence located above his newspaper shop at Hyde Park.

Uncle Gordon was his Dad's brother whom he didn't think his Mum and Dad had a lot to do with. He thought it was really good staying in London.

The family went to Windsor Castle, Buckingham Palace, the Tower of London and heaps of other places that Peter didn't really remember. Peter and his brother, Anthony, thought the best part of staying in London was staying above the newspaper shop, where their uncle allowed them to read all the comics on the shelves, so long as they were careful, didn't crease them and put them back on the shelves when finished, and playing with their, newly discovered cousin, twelve year old Billy.

Then on the fourth day, it was onto another train for a twenty eight mile trip from Hyde Park to Tilbury Docks to board the Orient Line's ship the SS Orontes, which was bound for Australia.

It seemed to Peter to take all day once off the train than to go through this big warehouse type of building where people were in queues to go through customs in order to board the ship and the crowd, there was no way all these people were going to get onto this ship.

After what seemed forever, the family finally emerged at the other side of the building where this huge ship was waiting beside the dock that swarmed with even more people that were in the building. They had exited from the customs building and onto the gangplank of the ship, wow what an experience, he had never seen such a big ship.

It must have taken at least an hour to get from the bottom of the gangplank to board the ship waiting in the long queue, then finally on board and his father presented the passage tickets to the steward who issued keys and a map showing the cabin locations that were allocated to the family.

They had one cabin, consisting of four single bunks for Peters's mother and the three children, then another berth in a cabin shared by three other males for his father. Another steward was dispatched to accompany the family as a guide to the cabin on E deck.

It was pretty sparse accommodation, with four single bunks, one small table, two chairs and two small easy chairs. On the table there were various pamphlets, including sitting times for meals and also the ships itinerary, this showed the ship leaving on that day 7th of September, arriving in Gibraltar on the 10th Sept, Naples 13th Sept, Port Said on the 16th Sept, Aden 20th Sept, Colombo 26th Sept then Fremantle on the 4th October. Fremantle was the Harris family's destination.

Peter was fascinated and just could not wait for it all to happen. But first, up to the promenade deck to watch the ship's departure from England.

The deck was packed with passengers waving farewell to friends and relatives that may never be seen again and were holding streamers of many different colours between them. Peter's family had no friends or relatives on the dock to wave to, but they all still waved into the crowd of strangers.

Having finished waving left no time for exploration of the ship as the time for the family's first dinner aboard the ship was looming and preparation for that had to be attended to first.

Peter had never been to a restaurant and was just amazed at the grandness of the dining room as he walked in with his family, then shown to their table by a steward who also seated them, issued and applied a napkin to each and then presented menus.

The menu took some working out, and was hard to read and was totally alien, not only to Peter but also to his mother and father, his siblings just had no idea.

Peter thought he could work out the 'Ham Soup' but asked his mother what the 'Halibut Creole' was. His mother could not answer and asked his father who replied whilst shrugging his shoulders, "fish". then Peter asked his mother if he would like 'Sirloin of Beef' as he couldn't remember ever eating beef, let alone sirloin.

Dinner was just a great adventure on its own, but he was blown away when he discovered they could have lemonade or orange juice to drink, as that only happened rarely at home in Blackpool, plus there were grapes, oranges, pineapple, other fresh fruit and tangerines wrapped in silver foil.

When it was found that ice cream was also an option for dessert, Peter's mouth just fell open, how good was this voyage going to be?

It was off to bed for all and Peter's father said goodnight as he headed off to his shared cabin, the rest of the family felt a little sad that father had to sleep elsewhere rather than with them but, his father did not seem to be upset at all, in fact he seemed quite happy.

His father also, Peter thought, seemed to sleep in on most mornings, as the family never saw him at breakfast.

The next morning a brochure was pushed under the door saying "Good Morning" and went on to announce all the events that would be happening on board that day.

Off to the first breakfast of the voyage and...wow, no porridge as the normal breakfast at home, but Rice Bubbles, Cornflakes, Pancakes, Bacon, Eggs, Braised Steak, Orange Juice, Pineapple Juice, Apple Cider, or just Iced Water.

It just could not get better, Peter was thinking as he started to explore the ship, only to discover that all the children aboard the ship get an ice cream at 10:00 am and 3:00 pm each day as well as lemonade and orange juice.

There were heaps of activities for the children on board including movies, pantomimes, live children's shows, deck games and swimming. There were also lots of other children to make friends with, and... every birthday child had a huge party and *all* the children were invited to attend.

It was on the second day out from Tilbury when crossing from the English Channel to the Celtic Sea, that the ship started to roll in the heavy swells, that Peter's mother, Mrs Harris, was, 'self' confined to her cabin due to sea sickness.

On the third day, the ship arrived at Gibraltar and as the Orontes was not docking at this port, she was met with a flotilla of small boats selling Spanish tourism merchandise. The ship dropped some passengers off, took on more water and fuel oil then away to the next destination.

It was on one of Peter and Anthony's ship exploring expeditions, that found them on C deck, that they came across a gentleman sitting on his own at one of the saloon tables with, what appeared to be, a draught board, on this board however, were not the run of the mill type buttons, but different objects that were placed neatly in rows. The man was intently staring over this board and some of the objects seemed to be out of place.

Peter could not help himself, he asked the man what were these objects.

The man, who spoke with a very strong accent, smiled and indicated to the brothers to sit down on the chairs on either side of him, which they did without taking their eyes from the strange objects.

Once seated the man explained that these objects were called 'chess pieces' and that the board was called a 'chess' board and together they formed a game of 'chess'. He then asked if they played, and then laughingly answered his own question, of course, how could they play the game if they didn't even know what the game was?

This man's name was Henri as the boys shortly discovered, and he turned the chess board around so that each end of the board with the figures in place, was in front of each brother. He then simply announced that he was going to teach them the game of chess. Strangely, both Peter and Anthony quite enjoyed their introduction to this game, so much, as did, apparently Henri, that it became an (almost) daily event for the entire voyage, after which both boys became reasonable players. They never did beat Henri though!

Naples, was another three days from Gibraltar, sailing through the Mediterranean and with much less rolling of the ship, allowed Mrs Harris some time on deck. At Naples, the family was able to leave the ship for the day to see the attractions that this Italian City, had to offer.

Peter's mother could not stop rocking and found it difficult to walk so the tour was cut short. That evening, the ship sailed to Port Said, which was also a three day journey.

It was here at Port Said, that Peter's father was looking forward to going ashore as he had been based here in 1956, whilst serving with the British Army during the Suez crisis, and was looking up some old friends who were still based there.

Mr Harris (Harold) had joined the British Army in 1947 after serving as First Officer in the British fleet of armed trawlers

Since joining the British Merchant Armed Fleet in 1940, he had gained his MED, then worked his way up to Ship's Mate.

Mrs Harris and the family stayed on board whilst Mr Harris headed off to see his old comrades. Mr Harris arrived back on board just before sailing, he must have had such an exhausting day as he fell asleep in our cabin and could not be woken till the next morning.

Arriving in Aden, just four days after leaving Port Said, the family spent the day around the shops and sightseeing in general. The ship sailed that night for Colombo, a six day journey.

During this time the seas were moderate and much time was spent on the ship's decks by all, including Peter's mother, who was starting to gain her sea legs, it's strange that none of the Harris family seemed to become seasick other than the mother. It was also during this time that Peter learned how to swim in the ship's pool that had previously been closed for swimming due to the rough seas.

Colombo was mostly remembered by Peter due to the extreme heat.

The family went ashore by an Indian launch, sailed by Indian sailors who were continuously chewing 'beetle nut' and spitting red stains on the Launch's decking. These Indian men with red stained mouths, would smile at the children and hold out their hands, jokingly, saying come with me, come, come! No way.

Mrs Harris organised two Rickshaws to take us all to the Gangaramaya Vihara Buddhist Temple, which seemed to take forever to get there and seemed to go through the middle of shops and homes, on the way.

Peter thinks that his mother may not have given enough in tips, as the ride back was so much quicker that it seemed to be only a couple of blocks to get from where they had started.

The ride was quite the highlight of the trip, although Peter did not have much interest in the Temple.

They found it just too hot and returned to the ship after only a few hours.

The Ship, having been re watered, food replenished and fuel oil taken on, all by barge, sailed on time, bound for the longest leg of the voyage, to Fremantle Australia, an eight day voyage. After the first two days, they crossed the Equator and all enjoyed the special festivities that go with crossing the Equator.

The following day the seas turned rough again and Mrs Harris was again committed to her cabin. It was around this part of the voyage that documentary movies of different Australian Cities were shown each day in the ships theatre.

This part of the voyage, especially the last three days, seemed to be the worst, the drinking water turned brown and all were advised not to drink it. Ice was no longer served in any drinks; things disappeared from the lunch tables like grapes, apples, and ice cream. Things also disappeared from the menus, such as steak and fish.

CHAPTER 6

The Destination

It wasn't only Peter that had felt he'd had enough of being on the ship, it also seemed everyone on board felt the same way. Even the ship's company didn't seem as friendly.

Then, early morning on day eight from Colombo, the Orontes sailed into Port Fremantle and up to Victoria Quay, where she docked in front of the customs shed amongst the cargo sheds

This should have been our 'destination', the end of our 'voyage', but two days earlier at sea, Peter's mother and father had watched a documentary about Western Australia, and in particular the migrant hostel in Perth, it seemed, to them, to be very rudimentary, nothing like the hostel in Sydney, that was shown in the New South Wales documentary.

It also seemed that the work in WA that Peter's father was more suited to, was very remote and could involve him living away from the family on work camps for extended periods.

Mr Harris had not very long ago, left the Army to be with his family and was not prepared to be away from his family for his occupation unless he really had to do so.

Mr Harris, who thought that he had very little hope with any chance of changing their disembarkation plans, consulted the purser with respect to change.

The purser informed him that there were in fact other families on board who also wanted to change from destinations on the eastern seaboard to the west, and vice versa and went on to say he was in touch with immigration on a daily basis once in Australian waters, and as the ship was here for four days, he would see what he could do.

Fortunately, a change was available with a family of identical numbers, and the change was made possible to disembark the Harris family in Sydney, New South Wales.

Peter did not know of this, he was only aware of this after being told the news by his parents that they were not getting off the ship here in Fremantle, as previously planned, but were now going to Sydney.

Peter, was actually rather sad as he was, at this point fed up with being on the ship, and even sadder when he learnt that it would be another nine days until the family would disembark at Sydney.

The journey from Fremantle to Adelaide meant, the ship had to cross The Great Australian Bight, known as a wild weather area for shipping, which also meant, it was back to the cabin for Mrs Harris.

It did seem to help that each city on this part of the final trip to Sydney, was only around two days sailing to each port, and a full day in each port Adelaide and Melbourne was in itself quite an adventure.

Another thing that seemed to help the boredom was that the coast could be seen all along the way, which was actually quite interesting.

The Harris family arrived at Piermont in Sydney Harbour, after disembarking and proceeding through customs, which took hours and hours, they were then, finally placed on a bus with a sign on the front of the bus displaying East Hills, sounds good, Peter thought as he boarded the bus with his family.

The bus trip of 25 miles through city streets, shopping centres, and towns, took almost an hour, an hour of discovering the Harris family's new surroundings and home, Australia. Unreal, let's do it!

The bus from Piermont with the Harris family on board, and about thirty other immigrants, pulled up front of the main hall and dining room at the hostel's administration oval park's dirt road, immediately upon stopping, the hostel manager jumped on board the bus and asked everyone to come into the main hall for registration.

The centre of the administration oval, was a park or playground, of sorts and sported what could be called a lawn. Peter and lots of other kids didn't go into the main hall but thought it better to wait, and play, on the grass.

Probably, after about one hour, the parents started coming from the hall and collected their bags that the bus driver had left on the path next to the hall.

Peter saw his parents with his sister in tow, emerge with the small crowd and head for their luggage.

Peter quickly found his brother Anthony and went up to his mum who was holding a bunch of documents in her hand. His dad was holding two keys on a ring and tag in one hand, and staring at a map of the hostel (camp) in the other.

"This way", his father said and all followed, after about three minutes, they found number 32A, which was connected to 32B.

Although unknown at this stage to the Harris's, these huts were called Nissan Huts, and this camp was actually an ex army barracks that had been modified for family accommodation.

The huts were a half round building made from corrugated iron with an extending framed doorway, which was located about the centre, next to the neighbour's entry.

You entered the hut into a room about half the size of the whole hut with a small dinette and sink in one half, and a lounge area the other half, to the right were two bedrooms. Very basic to say the least with one double bed and two single beds, in the lounge was a night and day three seater lounge and two easy chairs. The kitchenette consisted of a table and four chairs, we needed five chairs, and that was the Harris family's new accommodation. For now anyway, hostel accommodation was temporary staging for migrants and their dependents for three months and up to twelve months in special circumstances.

Mrs Harris sat down at one of the kitchenette chairs and looked sad enough to cry, her husband, Harold attempted to console her but did not really know what to say or do.

Meanwhile, both Peter and his brother Anthony were beside themselves with excitement, and asked if they could go exploring, Mr Harris, said they could go, but to be careful and to be back by five o'clock for dinner at the canteen.

Peter could not believe how lucky they were to be able to live in such a place as this. It didn't take Peter and his brother very long to find the mysterious jungle (scrub) behind the camp and the fascinating, swimming spot at Williams Creek, through the bush on the other side of the camp. Before they knew it, it was time to get back for dinner.

Dinner at the canteen was another great adventure in the eyes of the brothers. The family was allocated a table at which to take all meals, there was a choice of foods that were collected and placed on your plate on your tray as you walked past the serverey. Peter's dad exclaimed that it was "is just like friggin armi", but all the kids thought it was just magic, you got a choice of what food you wanted, you could have the roast pork with just potatoes if you like, you didn't have to have cabbage or carrots, what a ripper! And you could go back for more sweets (dessert) if you wanted.

The family were back at 32A and just settling down, and with very excited talking from both Peter and his brother, Mrs Harris said "we haven't even got a radio to listen to", when there was a knock at the hut's one and only door.

Peter's dad answered the door to a fellow selling new electrical goods and asked if he could show them what most of the people who lived at the hostel bought from him. He made a few trips from his van to inside our hut bringing in different items each time.

The first item he said, was a must, and produced an 'Hecla' electric jug, followed by a 'Sunbeam' two door toaster then a 'Sunbeam' electric frypan and a 'Motorola' radio and then brought in a two bar 'Hecla' electric heater.

Mr Harris negotiated with the salesman and bought every one of the items and also ordered a 'Halsrom Silent Knight' refrigerator, it seemed to Peter that life was just getting better and better.

The next day was Saturday; Mrs Harris took Anthony and Marilyn with her to the shopping centre at East Hills. It was quite a walk to East Hills from the hostel over the Georges River footbridge. Mr Harris and Peter accompanied them into East Hills and then caught a train to Revesby where Mr Harris bought a second hand 1954 Holden car for £900.

It was a pale green car with dark green coloured vinyl seats, unreal thought Peter as he and his father got hopelessly lost trying to find their way back to East Hills.

Mr Harris found the Panania Hotel near the Railway Station and went in to ask for directions to East Hills, after about a half hour he brought a glass of lemon squash and a bag of crisps (chips) out to Peter and said he wouldn't be long and went back to the bar for more directions, as Peter ate his crisps he thought, how good is Australia, it just gets better.

It was starting to get late when Mr Harris finally found his way back to East Hills, it seemed that it was not very far from Panania but it seemed to take a while, and two lemon squashes for Peter, to get the correct directions from the pub, which did not work anyway, but finally they arrived safely.

Although Mrs Harris, at first seemed quite upset with Mr Harris, who told her

that he had only drunk a couple of beers whilst asking for directions, but she became quite calm and somewhat excited when looking at their new car and all was forgiven.

The canteen by that time had closed, but Mrs Harris had made toasted sandwiches for everyone, using her new electric frypan, she commented that once the fridge arrived we could eat more food at the hut rather than going to the canteen. Peter liked the idea of the canteen better, but he didn't comment.

Sunday had to be, of course a ride in the new car.

The kids in the back thought it was great, except for Peter's little sister, who at five years old was placed in the middle between Peter and Anthony and was much too small to be able to see through the car windows. A seat change was ordered by their mother and Marilyn was placed next to a window, which resulted in her being quite happy but not so Anthony.

Peter thought they were heading towards Sydney, and not long after they had just made a turn, they were stopped by a policeman who was driving a black Ford, with a blue light on the roof of the car.

The policeman advised Mr Harris that when making a right hand turn, into another street, he must go around the marker that is placed in the middle of the road, rather than turn before the marker, he then asked for his driver's license.

Mr Harris handed his driver's license to the police officer and was then asked if he knew that his license was not valid in Australia, to which Mr Harris answered that he had wondered about that, and added: "Thee tell yer bout every bloody thing ter do with Australia, but thee don't tell yer bout bloody license an a never really thort, you no".

The policeman was really nice and said, "Not to worry mate" and he told Mr Harris how and where to go to get his New South Wales driving license, but he also advised on, not driving around too much until he got his license fixed up!

So they drove back to the hostel with Mr and Mrs Harris in deep conversation.

It was still only just after midday when they returned to the hostel and Peter announced that he wanted to go swimming in the creek at the swimming spot he had found, Anthony, of course, was going with him, according to Anthony, and they both went looking for the shorts they had worn for swimming on the ship, then with their parents permission, and orders to be home by four o'clock as there was a roast dinner on at the canteen that evening.

Peter and Anthony could not believe the amount of people swimming in the creek, but they still jumped in and had a great time and also met some other kids who became good friends.

There were plenty of tractor and truck tyre inner tubes, being used as rafts and pontoons and they were both soon playing on these with their new friends.

Peter observed some kids paddling canoes, the canoes were 'home made' looking, from a sheet of corrugated iron that was folded in half with a strip of wood nailed in between at both ends. Peter made a mental note that he would make one of these.

Peter, asked one of the boys with the corrugated iron canoe where he got the iron from, he was told the Holsworthy Army Camp dump, you get lots of good stuff from there, he said, army hats, bullet cases, parts of uniforms, all sorts including old roofing sheets. Peter was very keen and asked the boy to show him how to get there.

The boy, whose name, after the introductions, was Carl, agreed and they planned to go there one day, but a Saturday would be the best, as it takes a while to get there and going after school just does not give enough time to get there and look through the stuff that has been thrown out. He also warned Peter that people were not allowed to go there, so to keep it quiet and hope they didn't get caught. Sounds even better, thought Peter, so be it!

The next Monday morning, the boy's mother, left Marilyn at the hostel's crèche and then went with them on the school bus to Hammondville Primary School to enrol both Peter and his brother Anthony, into the school.

The school registrar, having enrolled both boys, said that it was now a bit late in the day to start school and would be disruptive to the relative classes, so they would start school tomorrow morning at 9:00 am, and get here at ten minutes to nine o clock, for the morning assembly. All done

The walk back to the camp was about one and a half miles and took about an hour in the hot sun. They got back about midday just in time for the arrival of the fridge, once the delivery guys had placed in the kitchenette, where Mrs Harris wanted it, then plugged it in and said it would take about an hour to get cold.

Mrs Harris filled various containers that she had been collecting and placed them inside the refrigerator, then took the boys for a walk to the East Hills shops to buy some cordials to make drinks. Once at the shops, their mum bought them, their very first milkshake, of which both Peter and Anthony totally agreed, was just the best.

The next day was to be their very first day at an Australian school.

Peter had loved going to his last school at Grange Park Estate public school, in England. It was a very new primary school that was within a short walking distance of their English home, and he often rode his bike there. He really enjoyed many subjects at school but mainly history, grammar and manual arts, which included woodwork and leatherwork.

He also enjoyed the hot meals that were provided in the school dining room at lunchtime.

Peter's teacher in England, Mrs Shaw was just so lovely and very kind. When she discovered that Peter was going to Australia, she put on a whole week of lessons about Australia for the whole class. The lessons were mainly about Lt James Cook who discovered Australia, she spoke about the penal colonies. Bloody hell, thought Peter, convicts. Mrs Shaw went on to teach the class about the first fleet that arrived at Botany Bay with convicts from England to establish the first settlements in Australia.

So, now, what is this Australian school going to be like, Peter wondered.

Tuesday morning, the boys were up and dressed for school in their old English school uniforms, basically just wool blend grey serge shorts, pale grey cotton drill shirt and black leather shoes, it was too hot for jumpers so they were left off. Their mother had bought for each of them at East Hills yesterday a small brown suitcase type, school bag to carry their lunches in and whatever else they may need once they started school.

Saying goodbye to their mother they both headed to the canteen for breakfast and to collect their school lunches from the canteen then onto the school bus, which left at eight o'clock sharp.

As they both entered the canteen carrying their school bags, a loud voice broke the subdued mutter of people eating breakfast, "No ports in here"!

Peter said "What" to the lady who called out, and she told him not to give her cheek.

An English lady, sitting close to where the boys were standing, said in a nice, friendly voice. "She means your bags boy's, they call them 'ports' here".

They thanked her and obediently took their bags back outside, it was here that they saw a heap of school bags placed in the rack on the porch. Didn't see them on the way in!

Both boys enjoyed their breakfast. Peter did not understand his parents not being too keen on the food served at the canteen, as he really thought it was quite good.

After breakfast, they picked up a brown paper bag each from a table bearing a sign *'school lunches'*.

These brown paper bags were folded over at the top, both opened the bags to look inside, to find there were what seemed to be, two sandwiches, a piece of cake and an apple. Neat!

Waiting at the school bus stop, which was a shelter type of thing with one bench, other kids were using their school bags (ports) as wickets and were playing cricket, in which both Peter and Anthony instantly joined into the satisfaction of the other boys. Peter thought this is going to be all right here. The bus arrived and took them all to school.

All the kids, once at school, took their bags and placed them on the bag racks in front of their designated classrooms. Peter and Anthony had no idea where they would be, so they just carried their bags. The assembly bell rang and the two boys just followed suit with the other kids.

The Headmaster of the school stood on the concrete podium and a girl raised the Australian Flag on the flagpole, once raised, the Headmaster said, "The National Anthem" and the whole school sang God Save the Queen. Wow that was really good, we never did that in England.

Once the Anthem had been sung, the Headmaster said, "Good morning boys and girls. The whole school sang out "Good morning Mr Perry".

"Mr Bretts is sick today, continued the headmaster, "and Mr McBrace, will be taking class 3c with class 3a. We will be taking lunch one half hour early today to conduct an Emu Parade before lunch. Make sure you wash your hands following the parade. That's all, dismissed"!

The boys had no idea where to go so they went to the admin building (shed) where, they were, with their mother yesterday. The registrar was not there, but the secretary asked why they were in the office. The boys told her it was their first day at school and she then asked their names. Anthony Harris and Peter Harris replied the boys, the secretary then looked their names up in the allocation book, and told them, Peter 4b and Anthony, 3a. Off you go, and look smart or you will be late.

Peter found his classroom in the large shed type building and gingerly knocked on the door, "Come in" said about twenty voices in unison, followed by a single, authoritative, voice "DO YOU MIND!, I, am in charge of this classroom, NOT YOU"!

Then, the authoritative voice said, loudly and clear, "COME".

Peter, cautiously, opened the door, which swung towards him, and then stepped inside pulling the door closed as he entered, to see about twenty faces staring at him.

Peter did not notice the teacher standing at the corner of the room directly opposite the entrance, as the glare from the window directly behind the teacher, obscured his vision, until a booming voice emitted "AND, YOU ARE"?

Caught, completely off guard, Peter meekly replied "What".

"I said, W H O A R E YOU"? Whoever you are, you seem to be of poor hearing"

"I am Peter," said Peter, a little louder but even less confident.

"Peter........whom,......and, what do you want in here" replied the teacher, "have you come in here to tell me something? Or are you lost?"

Peter, becoming shy and nervous as he could feel all eyes in the classroom were upon him, said, as strongly as he could;

"I'm Peter Harris and I am new here, it's my first day, and sorry I'm late"

The teacher introduced himself to Peter as Mr Anderson, but you call me Sir. He then said, there are already too many Pommies in this class, I don't really know what I have done wrong in this school, he said.

Firstly, take your port outside and put it on the racks, then sit next to Phillips, over there, where I can keep an eye on you as I don't like your looks.

The whole class was laughing, loudly at Peter's expense, which caused him embarrassment as he thought he must be in trouble at the very first meeting of his new teacher. The previous teachers, he had in England were all nice lady teachers, there was only one male teacher who taught manual arts at his last school.

After a little while, sitting next to Phillips, who told Peter his name was 'Greg' and not to worry about 'Sir' as he was only joking and that he was always like that with new kids and added that he was really a 'good sort of bloke'.

The class broke for recess and all mustered outside in the open where bottles of milk were being distributed to the school children. Peter asked Greg, what is with the milk? And Greg told him they all get one every morning.

Peter tasted the milk and found it was foul, it was so warm as all the milk crates had been delivered early in the morning and had been sitting in the sun until ten o clock, the time for recess. Greg told Peter that he could buy a flavoured straw at the canteen, and that's what he did, as he also did not like the taste of warm milk.

Mr Anderson asked Peter to stand up and tell the class who he was, where he came from and what he knew about Australia, to which Peter did, but when Peter spoke of Lt Cook and discovering Australia and, the first penal colonies in Tasmania, he blew Mr Anderson away with his knowledge of Australian history.

Mr Anderson said that he was very impressed with Peter and that he could become a good example to the rest of the class. The rest of the class didn't seem to appreciate this, but after a while, Peter seemed to fit in with them.

Peter met other boys, and girls, that also lived at the hostel and had already made plans to get together later that day back at the hostel.

Lunchtime at school was at one o 'clock for half an hour, but today was an Emu Parade, of which Peter had never heard of.

Peter stayed with his new friend Greg, who introduced Peter to Tom and Wayne, whom he said were 'mates' of his. They all stayed together for the Emu Parade and showed Peter what to do. All that was involved was everyone (school students) lined up from the start of the school office, side by side, stretched out their left arm and all faced in one direction. Upon the order of the monitoring teacher, all walked slowly forward, bending down and picking up any rubbish that lay in their path.

When it was over, Peter ate his lunch with his new friends, they all ate lunch together in the big lunch shed.

Peter opened his lunch bag, he had already eaten the apple on his way to school on the bus, as did all the other kids, and he had eaten his cake at recess, so now it was time to eat the sandwiches. Yuk! said Peter, after taking the first bite of one of the sandwiches. Is it horrible, Greg asked, what was wrong with it and asked for a taste and declared it to be OK, it's just fish paste, Greg said.

Peter discarded the fish paste sandwich and tried the second sandwich, it tasted nice, but he didn't know what it was and handed the other half of the sandwich to Greg. Greg opened the half sandwich for inspection, then declared it to Devon, then promptly ate the sandwich.

That was the end of Peter's lunch, he was now really missing the English school's hot lunch.

Mr Harris had found employment as the skipper of a Sydney ferry on the Circular Quay to Milsons Point, then the Balmain run. He was on the afternoon shift, which started at noon and concluded at 9:00 pm each weekday and he had the weekend free, except when he was called in to work on the Taronga Zoo run, on either Saturday or Sunday.

Although the remuneration and security for this job were excellent, this was never going to be a permanent job for Peter's father for two reasons, it was too far to travel from East Hills and took too long through the heavy traffic, for one and the second was, to get a home and move from the hostel nearer to his work was much too expensive, and to buy an affordable, home in the newer suburbs like Kingswood or Penrith, made it much too far to travel. Not to mention the fact that Mr Harris found the job extremely boring.

School was going well for the boys, except for the first day at school for Peter, who was given detention for not paying attention and having to walk the hour home from school and getting into more trouble by worrying everyone about his whereabouts. Peter vowed never to do it again. It was a hot summer in 1959 at East Hills and much time was spent by all at Williams Creek swimming hole.

At the very start of the school holidays, Carl came around to Peter's hut and knocked on the door, Peter's mum answered the door and Carl asked if 'Pete" was home. Peter's mother, very indignantly, said that no one, with that name, lived here, but added do you mean Peter? Peter's, mum, did not like the nickname for Peter.

Carl, Peter and Anthony headed off to the Holsworthy army barracks dump site.

Carl led the way by following Williams Creek, through the bush, all the way to under the Heathcote Road bridge, then over the creek and a bit further up to the barracks fence. Carl was looking along the fence line for the hole, that he had previously been through to enable access to the rubbish dump. Having found the hole, all three worked their way through the thick scrub and bush towards the dump.

No sooner had they entered the army rubbish tip, but an army truck roared up to them and soldiers alighted from the truck and stopped them.

Without saying a word to the three boys, the soldiers put the boys into the back of the truck and one of the soldiers, sat in the back with the boys as the truck sped off.

To say that these boys were, terrified, would be an understatement, they didn't even speak to each other, and they had not a clue of what was going to happen but it wouldn't be good.

The truck came to a halt at the entrance gates to the Holsworthy army barracks, the soldier in the back of the truck opened the tailgate of the truck, got out and helped the boys out. The driver of the truck was already out of the truck and was pointing at the entrance gate. Without a word, the three boys left the barracks and walked home silently, never to enter the army barracks again.

It was the end of the brother's dream to build their own canoe from corrugated iron, but a huge surprise came on Christmas morning when they discovered a brand new, two man kayak, complete with two paddles, compliments of Santa.

It was a different Christmas in December 1959 in Australia, for many reasons.

There was no snow nor freezing weather, rather it was extremely hot at around 97°F during the day and was not much cooler at night. There was no family, relatives or friends, to visit, or visiting.

The Christmas, spirit, however, was alive around the camp and at the canteen whom, put on such a great Christmas lunch, and dinner that day, that the Harris family had a great, first, Australian Christmas.

CHAPTER 7

The First Move

I was late January, that Harold Harris mentioned to his deckie at work, that he was not too keen on driving this ferry for much longer, and would most probably be looking for another job soon. The deckie said, that a mate of his, who was also a deckie, was on a tug that was working at the Pittwater and the skipper had just suffered a medical condition and that the owners were looking for another skipper.

Mr Harris, obtained the phone number of the tug's owner, through his deckie's contact and called him the following Saturday. His name was Larry Kime, he and his brother Dennis, operated a road construction company and also a dredging company.

They were at present looking for a skipper for their tug that was used in connection with their dredge. Mr Kime went on to say that if Mr Harris was interested they could meet tomorrow, Sunday as it was the only time available for Mr Harris.

It was agreed to meet at the Newport Arms Hotel, at Pittwater on Sunday at 12:00 noon. Peter's father suggested the whole family should go there for a drive and have lunch out.

What a great drive it was to Pittwater, what a beautiful place and all the flash houses on the hills, overlooking the water, which was covered in boats of all kinds, wow, this was the place we should be living at, Peter's mother said whilst selecting and pointing out the homes she would like to live in. Finding the Newport Arms was pretty easy.

Mr Harris left the family in the car with a promise of not being too long, he was only gone for about twenty minutes and returned grinning. Peter's dad told everyone to come into the pub's 'beer garden' for lunch none of us had any idea, what a 'beer garden' was.

What a different place this 'beer garden' was, men and women, some with their children, were sitting at tables with big umbrellas, enjoying drinks or eating food. There was also a separate area for children to play.

They found a table and Mr Harris went into the bar to get drinks, he soon returned with Mr Kime and both were carrying drinks. Mr Kime introduced himself to Peter's mothers and nodded a "good day fellers" to the children, then added, "What are yous going to have for lunch, it's all on me".

Peter's mum, objected but Larry Kime would not hear of it! And insisted by suggesting the steak, chips and salad as the best choice today. Peter's sister Marilyn, said she wanted chicken rather than steak, to which Larry Kime said "No worries sweetie". But she ended up with a steak anyway, everyone did, and they were all cooked the same, medium.

Larry Kime did not stay for lunch, having bought the lunches he excused himself and said he would catch up with us a bit down the track, enjoy lunch, see ya's, and he was gone.

What a lovely person said Peter's mum, shame he couldn't stay. Mr Harris smiled and said that he also thought he was a nice fellow and straight to the point, he also added that he thought he would take up Larry Kime's offer to drive his tug.

Mr Harris, accepting Mr Kime's offer of the job as skipper at Pittwater, now meant he had two things that he must do. Find somewhere closer to live to Pittwater as it was nearly forty miles from East Hills, and then once accommodation at Pittwater was found, the next thing would be to tell the ferry service that he would be leaving. The whole family was super excited about this move.

Looking for somewhere to live near Pittwater was, sadly not Peter's job, but he tried to take a very active part, by choosing a mansion on the hill looking over the boats on the harbour. His suggestion however was dismissed and after some considerable time, it was decided to buy a caravan and live on the caravan park at Terry Hills, just nine miles from Pittwater, perfect.

The next day, Monday, Both Mr and Mrs Harris went out looking at caravans at Parramatta, before Mr Harris had to start work at midday. They found a very large, twenty four foot, caravan and bought it, the next day was planned for a visit to Terry Hills caravan park and to organise to get the caravan towed there.

Everything went just as planned with no apparent drama, the boys were still on school holidays until 30th January and would simply start at another school for the 1960 school term.

The following Sunday, the Harris family said their goodbye's to their, just made, friends at the East Hills hostel. Their bags were packed and in the car, minus the kayak which had been sold to a friend of Anthony's, and minus the refrigerator which was sold to new arrivals at hut 38B.

The caravan had been towed to the caravan park at Terry Hills and all was ready to move in, quite a simple move really, though not as big as the hut, this big caravan, which actually slept six people, was comfortable for the whole family and Peters mum just loved it. Although it was only a very short time at the hostel, she did not like the hut nor the hostel facilities, especially the amenities and laundry…and..of… course, the food at the canteen.

The Terry Hills caravan park was located in a very quiet area on Mona Vale Road, although it was also surrounded by bush, this was much different as it was more like a rain forest. It was like heaven compared with the hostel, here you would actually have to go looking to find another person, rather than people everywhere at the hostel.

The Terry Hills public school was in Cooyong Road, about a one and a half mile walk, from the caravan park and a shop at Duffy's Forest about a mile further on.

The main shopping area was at Mona Vale, about six miles from the park. Mr Harris had only a nine mile drive to his work, which he thought was great and Mrs Harris was in no rush to find work and was content staying at home. Marilyn was due to start school that year, and Mrs Harris intended to walk her there and back each day.

Some of the film crew from the 'Whiplash' TV series, starring American actor Peter Graves, were also staying at this caravan park and told the boys that they had been filming scenes just over the road from the park.

More places to explore, Peter thought. Just over Mona Vale Road was an interesting looking place to start with, Peter saw wallabies as he walked through the forest and as he started to climb up a hill saw that he was actually walking over a rock with an Aboriginal etching of a kangaroo.

One day when Peter and Anthony were out walking past Duffy's Forest, just past Terry Hills, they discovered the Terry Hills golf club. Whilst wandering around there, just at the first tee, they saw two boys sitting on the bench and just as two golfers, pulling their golf buggies, stopped to tee off, the boys asked them if they wanted 'caddies'. The golfers must have said yes, as after the golfers teed off, the two young boys followed them, each pulling a golfers buggy.

This gave the boys an idea, after the golfers and the other two boys left, Peter and Anthony also sat on the bench in wait for more golfers. Anthony sat beside Peter on the bench and a lone golfer pulling a buggy came up to the first tee, Peter jumped up and asked if he wanted a caddy, the golfer said yes, so Peter started towing the golfer's buggy for him and told Anthony to wait for the next golfer and do the same.

After nine holes the golfer, whose buggy was being towed by Peter stopped at the clubhouse for a drink and bought Peter a coke, as Peter was drinking the coke, another golfer appeared at the clubhouse for a drink with Anthony in tow, carrying a big set of golf clubs. Anthony was shattered, it had been real hard work carrying those clubs, but thank goodness his golfer was only going nine holes. He gave Anthony two shillings.

Seeing the reward that Anthony received from his golfer, Peter was keen to get going when his golfer resumed for the next nine holes and upon completion gave Peter, two, two shilling, pieces. A bit disappointed, but still good, Peter headed straight back to the first tee again and found Anthony there, sitting on the bench.

Sitting next to Anthony on the bench, waiting to see if more golfers should arrive, they decided that if the golfers were carrying their golf clubs, then they would not ask them if they wanted caddies. They both got another caddy job together with the next set of golfer's and they each received a coke at halfway and five shillings each at the end. They were on a great thing and decided to call it a day and head home.

Both boys were very excited when showing their mother the nineteen shillings they had earned, but their mother looked at them very suspiciously and asked them exactly what they had done, the boys explained the caddying and their mother said that was alright for them to do that, but reminded them to be careful of strangers. The golfers on the course that day must have been very rich as all subsequent golfers that they caddied for, only gave them one, or sometimes two shillings for the whole eighteen holes. They soon became tired of being caddies and discovered better money in finding lost golf balls in the water hazards around the course, and then cleaning them in the golf clubs ball cleaning machine, one of the golfers showed the boys how to add sand to the ball cleaner to make it clean better. They were caught doing this by the greenkeeper and were banned from the course. Ah well, it was all good, until that happened.

Peter got the opportunity to go to work with his father on occasions, it was really good as he got to learn how to row the dingy from the jetty out to the tug. It was great on the tug, especially when they were towing the dredge, or moving it into position. When the tug was just tied alongside the dredge, Peter would fish from the deck of the tug. The tug had a crew of two plus Peter's father, who was the skipper and in charge of the tug, the dredge had a crew of two also, and all slept on the tug when operating, it was too far to come back to the wharf each day. The tug had a galley for eight people and some easy chairs, two cabins with four bunks in each, an amenities cabin with two toilets and two showers and a wheelhouse with a cabin at the back with a toilet and shower, table, chairs and bed for the skipper.

The dredge also had an amenities cabin, galley and accommodation cabins but they were only used to store equipment and not used for accommodation due to the poor condition they were in.

Mr Harris enjoyed working on the tug, as it was not monotonous work like the ferries and it was much better pay. The only drawback to this type of work was if the dredge could not work because of foul weather or rough seas, then the crew was laid off until the weather permitted the dredging to continue.

The family was invited to a party at Larry Kime's house on Prince Alfred Parade at Newport, right on the water's edge one Sunday afternoon.

The house from the front looked nice but pretty ordinary, the Harris family thought as they arrived, but as they walked what seemed a great distance, around to the back yard, where the party was being held, they saw the great views and the rest of the house and it just blew them away, wow.

There was a big covered patio area with tables and chairs with people chatting and drinking, a BBQ, which was the first time for the Harris's, with food cooking on it, a huge swimming pool with some kids swimming and a jetty with a great looking cabin cruiser tied to it.

Larry saw the Harris family arrive and welcomed them by saying "Hey! Grab a beer, Harry, what will you have Mary, kids help yourselves to whatever".

Harry? Who was Harry, they were all thinking, then it dawned on Peter's dad and he announced to the family that it looked like he had just been given a nickname, 'Harry'.

What a great day they all had, they met Larry's brother, Dennis, who seemed old enough to be Larry's father, and they also met Dennis's son, Steve, who was about seventeen years old and seemed really nice to talk to.

Peter and Anthony, went swimming and met the other kids in the pool, two of which were Larry's children, Jane and Brian. Following a swim it was time for lunch then Steve took all the kids for a ride in a big launch that was also tied at the jetty.

What a marvellous day, Peter thought, I wish I could live here in this house. The end of the school holidays were coming to a close and it was almost time to start another new school, Peter was not too enthused about going to school and neither was Anthony.

The day had come and the Mother enrolled the boys and Marilyn in Terry Hills public school, it was a lovely school and only about 10 years old with friendly staff and teachers. Peter really enjoyed this school, the teacher was a lady this time and was not as cranky as Mr Anderson had been.

Mrs Freyer was Peter's new teacher for his start of fifth grade primary school, as Peter was the only 'English' pupil in her class, she was interested to know about Peter's school in England and asked him to tell the class about his former school.

The whole class was quite interested to listen and were just amazed when Peter told them about getting a hot lunch served every day at Grange Park Primary School.

One of the class said that it sounded a lot better than the warm bottle of milk that was made available at this school and went on to say, he couldn't understand why the crates of milk were always left in the hot morning sun when delivered every morning. It seemed that nobody knew why this was.

The months had rolled on to September and the winds had started to pick up, quite normal for this time of the year, so we were told. Sadly, gale force winds had set in and their father was unable to work for nearly a week and things weren't looking any better, no work meant no pay for Mr Harris, so he contacted Larry Kime and told him that this was no good to him and he would have to find work somewhere else. Larry told him that if he was prepared to travel, then he had work for him operating an excavator on the Pacific Highway extension at Ourimbah, about 50 miles from Terry Hills, just over an hour's drive. Mr Harris was happy with that and said he would be there next Monday to start.

At this time, Peter's grandmother was coming over to Australia from England and arriving mid next year, and Mr and Mrs Harris had been contemplating selling the caravan and looking for a house to rent, as they would now require more room for the grandmother's arrival, now this seemed the perfect time to move closer to Ourimbah and Lakes Entrance looked good.

Mr Harris's deckie, who was also off work due to bad weather, offered to tow the Harris caravan with his Ford F250 truck to the Blue Lagoon caravan park at Bateau Bay, just down the road from Lakes Entrance. So it was a pretty simple move, we came home from school on the Friday and moved to Bateau Bay, on Saturday 8th October 1960, pretty cool spot Peter thought, as he checked out the beach that was right next to the park on the following day. This was a much better looking place to live than Terry Hills, both Peter and Anthony agreed. And, there was a golf club next door.

All the Harris children had a week off school, the following week, as Mrs Harris was too busy unpacking things. The children did not complain.

CHAPTER 8

Bateau Bay

The first week at Bateau Bay, was just unreal, Peter and Anthony discovered that they could walk on the beach and follow the shore from Shelly Beach, where the caravan park was to Blue Bay Beach then on to North Entrance Beach, it was about 3 miles and there were heaps of rocks to walk over and rock pools to discover.

Most mornings found a few surfboard riders on the beach, which both boys watched in fascination, they became friendly with some of them and it was not long before both were surfing on a borrowed board from a man at the caravan park. It was a very heavy and old fashion surfboard, made from beechwood framing and plywood top, bottom and sides. It was a very big board and both could ride on it at the same time, it was great fun, but it must have slowly leaked water into the inside which made it sluggish and when they got washed off it, then it was very hard to get get it back to shore.

Just around the south point of Shelly Beach was Bateau Bay Beach, a quiet little cove with little, if any surf. Here the boys found an old man with a donkey harnessed to a single axle cart with rubber tyres, he was shovelling sand onto the cart and of course, the boys approached him and asked if they could help.

The man simply gave the boys his shovel, then sat down on the beach as the boys shovelled sand onto the cart, until the boys said, they'd had enough, whereas the man took back his shovel and recommenced shovelling sand onto the cart.

The boys continued their exploration journey, going south on the amazing rocks and pools around Crackneck Point, the accessible shoreline went on and on.

It was amazing to look into the rock pools and attempt to catch the fish that was trapped in them. They were warned by other people on the rocks, to start to get back around the point as the tide was coming in and they could get stuck there.

Peter and Anthony headed back the way they had come and when back on Bateau Bay Beach, saw the old man with the cart and donkey, sitting on the beach whilst some other people were shovelling sand onto the cart. Peter wondered if the old man, actually ever did very much shovelling himself.

There was an old boat lying upside down on this beach, just near where the man and the donkey were located. Peter asked the old man if it was his boat, to which he answered that the boat had been there since before he had moved to Bateau Bay, some three years back, as far as he knew it was just abandoned as it was probably useless. Peter thought that this may be a good project for the future.

It was another, new start, at the local school for the Harris children. Mrs Harris had taken all three by the local bus service to The Entrance public school and all went quite well, Marilyn was in first class, Anthony, in fourth class and Peter was in fifth class, another getting used to a different school system, meeting new friends. Peter had been in Australia for just over a year and had now been enrolled in three different schools. They seemed to teach different stuff in each school but in the same school grade, strange.

The Entrance primary school was three miles from the Bateau Bay primary school which was not too far for Peter and Anthony to walk, but much too far for their sister Marilyn, so, the school bus was taken by all three, to and from the school each day. This later, was to the to annoyance of the boys who had met new friends at school and wanted to spend time with them after school, but they had to escort their younger sister on the school bus.

They cunningly organised a roster where they would take it in turns to travel home on the school bus, perfect, until, the first week of the roster they became a bit confused and on the Wednesday neither of the boys was there to escort Marilyn.

The wrath of this from their mother results in the demise of the roster system.

It was December 16th, 1960. The start of the school holidays, until 30th January 1961. The caravan park at Bateau Bay became packed with campers for the Christmas holiday period.

Peter and Anthony had big plans for these holidays.

The Shelley Beach golf club didn't seem to mind the two boys doing caddying and there always seemed to be customers for them and it seemed they were making around between 8/- and 10/- each day between them, plus their second hand golf ball business of around 2/- per day, meant it was not long before they had saved up the ◇3/10/- that was required to buy a second hand fibre glass surfboard that a school friend of Anthony's was selling.

It was a balsa core, fibreglass longboard and although it was of very rough appearance and most probably older than the boys themselves, and had been repaired a bit, they thought it was magic and soon the old plywood surfboard was abandoned as with the caddying at the golf club.

The surfing had been causing many fights between Peter and Anthony, because one of them, or both, were having longer turns on the board than the other, and the other, old, board could not be used, as it took two of them to handle it.

The coming of Christmas 1960 at Bateau Bay, was a great time for the Harris family and also resolved the boys' surfing problems with Santa Claus, bringing a new surfboard to Anthony and a set of snorkelling gear to Peter and a buoyancy vest each for the two boys. Happy Christmas.

The new surfboard was pretty well taken over by Peter. This was because, as Peter said to Anthony, this board is much too fast for you and is not safe. For some strange reason, Anthony believed Peter and seemed happy just to have the old surfboard to himself. Peter thought himself to be very considerate of his younger brother and now had a new surfboard and snorkelling gear.

Just after New Year, the Christian Youth Workers Australia set up a big tent, very close to the beach at the southern end of the caravan park, it was huge, a bit like a circus tent, but not as large. They invited everyone at the caravan park to their tent for an opening BBQ, the first evening the tent was set up and announced that the next morning there would be breakfast served for everyone who wished to attend and following that, there would be events for all on the beach.

The organisation of breakfast and beach events, by the Christian Workers, happened every single day for the whole week and Both Peter and Anthony did not miss one of them. The breakfast was mainly BBQ sausages on bread rolls and orange juice, the beach games consisted of volleyball, beach soccer, foot races and other events. The prizes for winners and runner ups, was mainly religious objects and items, such as pocket bible's, bookmarks and "I love Jesus" stickers. Everything they did was themed around religion, but not so heavy as to spoil it.

There were many new kids around Peter and Anthony's age who were holidaying

with their parents at the park and it was great to go surfing and playing with them at the beach. It was also a good opportunity, Peter thought, to check out the old boat on Bateau Bay beach, whilst they had a few friends with them to help.

It was quickly organised amongst them all and they proceeded to where the old boat was located. Even with seven boys, aged between eight to eleven years old, it was difficult to turn the old boat over to discover there were two, very old looking, oars lying under it, but no rowlocks. They dragged the boat to the water, together with the oars and commenced to push the boat into the water. All the boys were full of excitement at the prospect of rowing the boat around the cove, but very dismayed as the boat sank instantly it entered the water.

As the old man who was back at the beach again, with his donkey and cart, was watching this event unfolding, the boys decided to return the boat back to where they had found it. It was extremely hard to get the boat back up the beach now the boat was wet, and the beach was of course, uphill, they eventually succeeded in getting the boat back and turned it upside down with the oars placed under. All were exhausted, but all agreed that it had been a great time.

Just before the return to school, Mr and Mrs Harris were again considering the sale of the caravan and had been looking for homes to rent around the Bateau Bay, Long Jetty and The Entrance areas, to no avail as there was very little available to buy or rent within their budget. They had found, however a house for rent well within their budget, some fourteen miles from The Entrance at Buff Point.

Although Buff Point was to be a much greater distance for Mr Harris to travel for his work, he was prepared to stay at the work camp at his work site, for four nights a week and he would be home every Friday night and leave on Monday mornings.

Mr and Mrs Harris made the announcement to the family and the plans for the move were made. The caravan, being so large and in such good condition, did not take long to sell and was bought by people who were actually renting a caravan at the very same caravan park, which made things even easier. The Harris's had no furniture but there was some furniture that was available with the house at Buff Point for purchase. It seemed everything was going to make for a very easy move.

CHAPTER 9

Buff Point

The family loaded up the car, complete with the two surfboards on a roof rack that Mr Harris had fitted himself. They drove the fourteen miles to Moola Road, Buff Point.

The house at Moola Road, was a bit ramshackle, thought Peter. His mother, although having seen the home before they rented it, also looked a bit disappointed. But, Peter's dad, optimistically said, just wait till we clean it up a bit and it will be great. The house had a house name sign attached to the top of the front verandah that said *'Dunroamin'* and Peter said to his parents that he wished it to be true, whereupon his mother said, yes! No more moving.

Buff Point was, to Peter, quite disappointing when compared to Bateau Bay insomuch as the location of beaches, shops and schools. But!

This house was huge, it had three inside bedrooms and two sleep outs on one of the verandas, and two bathrooms, one being in the laundry at the back. Two big sitting rooms, a huge kitchen, a large dining room, laundry and two verandas, It was a very old house constructed from timber with fibre sheeting on the outside and unpainted masonite in most of the rooms, timber boards, that creaked quite loudly in places in the sitting and dining rooms and also pressed metal ceiling's with stamped pattens.

Spooky, thought all the children. Peter thought it was good that he could have his own bedroom. The bathrooms in the house also seemed to be quite large, each had a bath with a shower at one end, next to the shower and the taps for the bath was a water heater that required a fire to be lit for hot water, a chip heater, Peter's dad called it, there were two of them in the house, one each in the bathrooms, the kitchen had an electric hot water heater next to the sink and the laundry had a firebox under a huge copper. Peter's mother did not like this firebox in the laundry and bought an electric emersion heater to use instead. There was a large concrete tub that was divided into two big concrete sinks, one had a wooden mangle attached to it.

The stove in the kitchen was huge with an oven on each side of the burner box and hot plates the full length of the top, it was originally a wood burner but had been converted to oil. There was a large open fireplace in both sitting rooms that backed onto each other to share the chimney, there was also a fireplace in the dining room that backed onto another fireplace in a bedroom and two other bedrooms also had fireplaces backing onto each other, of which two of these had been blanked off. The house had three large brick chimneys for the fireplaces and two, round asbestos chimneys for the chip heaters.

The was a lot of needless, fighting amongst the children for the selection of bedrooms with fireplaces, but, Mrs Harris had already allocated the bedrooms with fireplaces and, none went to the children. So be it.

The house was on three quarters of an acre, the laundry was situated on the back verandah and there was an old garage beside the house, an abandoned chook shed was behind the garage. The toilet was just away from the laundry and it was called a "long drop" and the only description that everyone called it was "YUK". No one thought they would be using to toilet at night, no way!

There were fruit plus other trees scattered around the huge backyard with what seemed to be an old stable at the very end.

It was only a walk of around five hundred yards to the jetty at the lake and you could swim there with a little care. There was a general store just around the corner, on Bruce Road. The primary school was at Budgewoi which was only about less than one mile walk.

The primary school at Budgewoi was unbelievable, it consisted of only two buildings. The main building held the administration office and teacher's common room with staff toilets and three classrooms. Another building housed the boy's and girls' toilets and an open area for lunches and other activities for inclement weather. Each classroom catered for two grades from one to six.

This school had only three teachers and one headmaster, who doubled as a teacher if another was absent. It was quite different being in a classroom that was back to back, but with the same teacher.

All the Harris children, went up a grade when they started at this school. Peter found it strange that Anthony was in the same classroom as he, but it was a very friendly, dual class atmosphere with a great teacher who quite often combined both grades, which made learning quite enjoyable.

It was at the end of February 1961, that Peter's grandmother arrived on the ship Orsova at Piermont docks in Sydney. Mr and Mrs Harris, and daughter Marilyn, travelled the seventy miles to Sydney to collect her and her partner, Jack Higgins, to bring back home to live with us, hence to a large home that was rented at Buff Point.

Mr Harris had a job lined up for Jack, where he was working with the Kime Brothers earth moving company.

Peter and Anthony, were both missing their surfing as the closest beach was at Budgewoi, which was about three miles from their home and just too far to walk carrying their surfboards. They did however discover a VJ sailboat for sale in Buff Point that was in very good condition and, with their parent's permission, traded both their surfboards and three pounds, for the sailboat. The boys were ecstatic, the man they did the trade with, showed them how to insert the sail into the mast then step the mast and attach the boom, then run up the little jib sail, attach the sliding keel and the rudder and finally the tiller.

It did not have a spinnaker, as that had been stolen some time ago, said the man and he had no idea where the pole for it was either. He then showed them how to de rig the little boat and pack it ready for travel

It was quite light but it took both boys to lift the boat, one at each end, with the boats wooden boom, sail battens and mast on the top and sails in a bag, also on top, they both started to struggle towards the gate with the boat.

The man looked at them, bemused and said, "Don't you's want its trailer"? I only took it off the trailer to make it easier to show you how to rig it.

Peter, nor Anthony, had realised that the boat also came with a small boat trailer. Wow! Another win. The man also explained that it could be transported on a car's roof bars, or rack, but the trailer made it much easier. He showed how it went onto the trailer and said to the boys to get hold and lets drag it to the lake for a demo.

After demonstrating again, how to rig the VJ and which rope did what and so forth and then the sailing technique, the man, on his own, headed off in the boat and had made it look so easy when he sailed it around in front of them.

He showed them how to learn to sail in a circle, and if they could accomplish this, he said, then they could sail in any direction and virtually sail anywhere. Peter thought, right this is our first task to learn. Then the man brought the boat back to the shore and said to give it a go!

They both carefully got aboard the little boat and it did nothing. The man said, pull slowly on the main sheet (meaning the rope attached to the boom) Anthony, sitting at the back near the rudder and main sheet, did as the man said and.....holy...jeeps, the little boat came magically to life and in an instant, took off away from the shore. "Ease up! Ease up, don't pull the sheet in so much, let it go" the man screamed at them, but, too late, the little boat had capsized and lying on its side with the boys beside it, where the mast lay in the water.

"Well, get around the other side" the man yelled "and get the bastard back up" he continued, "You have to jump on the keel, then grab the side and just pull back, both of you at the same time" he went on, and as the boy's efforts failed to right the boat back, he continued with "for Christ's sake put a bit of bloody effort into it, you useless beggars".

The boat's hull finally flipped back into the water. The boys were a bit shook up and started to push the boat back to shore when the man sang out, "What the hell are you doing, you won't learn that way, you silly buggers, get back on and have another go, you will never learn if you're frightened of it"

The boys got back onboard, dripping and a bit shaky, Peter was at the helm this time and pulled on the main sheet very slightly and nothing happened, then a little more and the boat moved very slowly, a little more sheet and the boat went a little faster. Right, Peter thought, this is how it's done, just as the man said "You've got it! Now, try tacking the other way by letting the sheet off and turn the tiller the other way. Over they went again.

The man was laughing loudly and said you should have life jackets on and was joined by other bystanders, who were also laughing. The boys now knew to get on the other side, and they had the boat back up in a flash. "Yous'll be right," said the man as he walked away, "enjoy your new boat, and don't forget the life jackets".

And that was how they learned to sail. They practised as the man had told them to sail around in circles, the circles got bigger and bigger as they got better and better. It wasn't long before they started exploring that lake, then the Tuggerah lakes, then racing any other boat they saw on the water. They were amazed that they could overtake most of the motorboats on the lake. They did have many spills also, but as the saying goes, many thrills also. This was definitely the life!

The fishing at the Buff Point jetty was just great, Peter caught Bream, Blackfish, Garfish and Longtoms, and even a couple of Flathead from time to time, he thought that fishing was just brilliant, especially when he took it home and his mother would cook it for the whole family.

Peter, had a school friend called Robert, but the kids at school called him Bobby. whose father had a fishing boat on the lake at Buff Point and was invited to go prawning with them one Friday night. The boat was a large open boat with what looked like, a large table with a large roller over the top at the back, directly in front of this table was a rolled net sitting at the bottom of the boat. The net had white cork floats at one end and lead weights at the other, these were spaced at about three feet for the entire length of the net, and the start of the net had a heavy weight attached.

The boat had a motor in the centre and also oars in front of the motor. As the boat got into position on the lake, Robert's father stopped the boat's motor and Robert took up his position on the oars as his father dropped the net's heavy weight overboard, he then slowly let out the net as Robert rowed in a straight line. When Robert's father said, OK, Robert started to row in a big circle back to where they had first put out the net. Once they had reached the net's weight buoy, Robert's dad started to pull in the net, slowly over the big roller with the help of Robert. Peter tried to keep out of the way and just watched the net to see what would emerge.

As soon as the net started to come over the roller, the prawns could be seen caught in the bag of the net, the prawns were removed from the bag and placed into a large plastic box. It was not long before the net was back in the boat and the plastic box had about a pound and a half of prawns, not real good said Roberts's father, Then it was away to do it again. After about two hours, three runs and about five and a half pounds of prawns, it was time to give it a miss tonight as it's a waste of time, said Robert's father, and we'll head back,

When they reached Robert's house, on the shore of the lake, Peter thought that was it for the night as it was about eight o'clock, but Robert said that they were now going to cook the prawns and that Peter could help. For sure, said Peter as he helped carry the box from the boat.

Robert's father had already started the gas boiler behind the house as the boys brought up the prawns. The gas cooker was very noisy and Peter thought that it must surely wake the neighbours. As soon as the water boiled, and made even more noise, the box of prawns was tipped into a basket in the boiler and the water started to simmer.

Once the water came back to the boil, Robert's father removed the basket of prawns and emptied the prawns into a huge tub of water with an ice block floating in it.

It was about eight thirty that Peter arrived home with half a pound of cooked prawns wrapped in a paper bag, that Robert's father had given him, saying "Give these to your old man".

Mr Harris had taken Jack Higgins with him to Ourimbah, and they would be back on Friday night.

It was only the day after they had left, on Wednesday that Peter's grandmother, said that she thought that, she may have seen a snake going under the firebox of the copper in the laundry, and that it had made her jump in fright.

When the children arrived home from school that Wednesday afternoon and was told about the snake, they wanted to check it out but were told, in no uncertain terms that they were not to go near the laundry.

Peter, had never seen his mum so shaken and frightened, they knew there were possums in the ceiling at this house, as you could hear them during the night moving around in the ceiling. They all knew there were mice in the house because everyone had seen one or two mice from time to time, but, this was the first snake, and it was inside the house, and, Mrs Harris was no longer happy.

Neighbours, who were a fair distance away from the Harris home, had warned that there are, from time to time, snakes around and that they are more active in these warmer months. Where their home was, about the middle of Moola Road, there were no other homes, it was sparse when it came to population in that area, most of the homes around Buff Point were around the lake.

Peter's mum asked him to go and see Mr O'Brien, at the corner shop in Bruce Road, and ask him what we should do.

Peter almost ran to the shop to tell Mr O'Brien and to ask for advice. Mr O'Brien did not seem to be alarmed whatsoever and calmly asked, the whereabouts of the snake. Peter, told him the laundry and that the door had been locked for the safety of all.

Mr O'Brien suggested to go back home and open the laundry door and that the snake would most likely be gone by morning. He also said, that the laundry door, the toilet door and any other outside facing doors should never be left open during the day, or at night, for that matter, as snakes will always take the opportunity to seek food, or water, in and around buildings.

Peter thanked Mr O'Brien, and starting to feel much relieved at the advice given by Mr O'Brien and he was sure his mother would also be relieved, he started to head back home as Mr O'Brien called out "Tell your mum, there was nothing to worry about, if left alone, that snake will go away" and then added "and tell her not to go looking for it as they can bite, and that is not good"

Feeling his mum would be delighted to hear this advice, Peter repeated what Mr O'Brien had told him. Peter's mother all but fainted and his grandmother, who was also listening intently, to what Peter was saying, went as white as a ghost and said "God Help Us All" to which Mrs Harris replied, *That is it!*

It was only two days until Mr Harris would arrive back home, and in those two days, everyone was on guard, no body went into the laundry, the door was shut fast, contrary to Mr O'Brien's advice, and nobody went to the toilet without Mrs Harris being with them, No One!

Mr Harris and Jack Higgins, arrived back at Buff Point, having made a detour to the Budgewoi Hotel, at about six thirty on Friday evening.

The moment Mr Harris walked into the house, Mrs Harris said "Harold, I have to talk to you, come this way please," as she walked him into their bedroom.

What is wrong! Jack Higgins asked Peter's grandmother, who simply put her right hand index finger to her lips.

Peter, could not understand why his mum had taken his father to the bedroom to talk as she could be heard quite clearly through the house. She had told Peter's father that the family was leaving Buff Point and that they were leaving as soon as practical, this weekend perhaps, but the family was not staying here any longer than necessary. She went on to tell him all about the snake but explained, that it wasn't that, she did not like living in the bush here in Buff Point.

She hated going to the toilet in the backyard, God knows what lived down that huge pit, she's fed up with the possums running around in the ceiling, which frightens her and makes her jump during the day.

At night it is so dark, there is no street lighting.

When she hangs her washing out to dry, it gets covered in dust from traffic driving down Moola Road.

It was too remote, she said, it was a long way to any decent shops and there was no bus service to speak about, she had no transport for doctors or hospitals, if anything happened to the children, the closet hospital was Wyong, thirteen miles away and she had no way of getting there.

The next morning, Saturday, Mr and Mrs Harris, were on their way back from Long Jetty following an inspection of a property in Gordon Street, which consisted of a three bedroom house and a two bedroom unit. Both the residences are furnished, which is also important as the Harris's were yet to own any furniture, as living in the hostel and a caravan, had not necessitated buying furniture.

The property was ideal, although much more expensive than Buff Point by almost double. It was, however, much more suited to the family and also perfect for Mrs Harris's mother and Jack, who were happy to pay half of the rent in return for the two bedroom unit. The homes were not as old as Buff Point, however, the toilets were still on the outside of the homes, as with the shared laundry. The toilets though were containers, rather than the long drop, which were collected by the council each week. The road at the front of the homes was bitumen and plenty of street lighting. Shops as close as one mile away at Long Jetty and plenty of busses to and from The Entrance. Definitely a winner, not to mention that the children go back to their previous school at The Entrance.

It was a very busy weekend at Moola Street Buff Point for the Harris family, but it didn't matter, as everyone was so happy to be going back near The Entrance, with the exception of the grandmother and Jack, who, of course, had never been there, but had heard so much about it from the children, that, they too were looking forward to the move. The only problem was the boy's little VJ sailing boat, Mr Harris's car did not have a tow bar, however, Robert's dad (the fisherman) had a tow bar on his ute and when asked, was delighted, he said, to take the little boat down to Long Jetty one day next week. So, everything is sorted, let's do it!

CHAPTER 10

Long Jetty

It was almost Peter's Birthday as the Harris family settled into the new house at Long Jetty. It was better than Buff Point by a mile, thought Peter, even though he had to share a bedroom with Anthony.

They were still next to a lake, and now even closer as Gordon Road was only one block from the lake, and there was only one house between them and Archbold Road, which went to the lake, right in front of the actual, 'The Long Jetty.'

Mrs Harris was so happy to be back in this area and her mother also thought it was a great place. Being only eight miles from Mr Harris's work meant that he, nor Jack, would no longer stay at the work camp but be home each night, another plus.

Back to the Entrance school was also good for the children as they had friends there from last term there. They were re enrolled at the school and all went into the next grade from when they were there last, so all had new teachers,

Peter's new teacher, was a fairly old man, when compared to the other male teachers at the school, and was also the deputy headmaster. His name was Mr Hastings, it seemed that Mr Hastings didn't really take to Peter at all.

It was a fairly short walk from Gordon Road to the public school at The Entrance, with a number of ways to go, Peters favourite was along the path at the lake shore to View Street which went directly to the school, it also passed Mr Hastings house. Peter often saw Mr Hasting at his house as he walked past and would wave and say hello. Mr Hasting either ignored Peter or simply glared at him. Peter changed his route from home to school to avoid seeing Mr Hastings.

Being sixth class (the one and only) there were various, weekly rosters in Peter's class, that all pupils were selected to do in rotation. One of these, that Peter seemed to get regularly, was 'ink monitor', which entailed being in the classroom, fifteen minutes early, every morning, to mix up the powdered ink into the large ink bottle with a rubber dispensing spout attached, then fill each and every ink well located in the desks in the class. There were about fourteen sixth class pupils, which meant that in a whole year, Peter should be the 'ink monitor' only three times a year. It seemed every day Peter, as ink monitor, filled the ink wells in the desks, he either overfilled or under filled the ink wells.

During the times that Peter was the 'ink monitor', each morning before the class would start, Mr Hastings would ask all the pupils, to check their ink wells, and report their condition, that is, were they filled properly, too full, too empty, or just correct.

Every pupil that reported other than correct, meant an extra day of 'ink monitor' duty. Peter was well aware that this did not happen to all 'ink monitors'. What can you do?

Mr Hastings was also well known for placing pupils on detention that was served by pupils weeding the lawn of his home a short distance from the school, and on one occasion he took a number of pupils on detention, to his bowls club to weed lawns.

The rumour was that one of the pupil's parents, seeing their child performing gardening duties at the bowls club, reported Hastings to the NSW Department of Education. The result was, that a new sixth grade teacher was incumbent by September that year. Goodbye Mr Hastings, and Peter resumed his original walking route to school.

Long Jetty was another just great location according to both Peter and Anthony and it certainly looked like a better lake for sailing their VJ,

The boys thought it might be difficult to get the VJ on it's trailer down to the lake, due to the short steep, section of the road, just around the corner on Archbold Road.

It was just too hard for the boys to hold back the trailer as they approached the bottom of the road, they found out the hard way, of course, things were going nicely, though the pressure was starting to build to slow down the trailer and it started to increase speed slowly, then it was getting, what the boys thought a bit too fast, then just as the boys were thinking of letting it go, a man who was walking past on Tuggerah Parade, grabbed hold of the front of the trailer in between the boys and brought it to a halt. It was close.

The boys thanked the man who had saved them, and the man asked where had they pushed the boat from. Peter explained that they lived just up directly behind the little shop on Tuggerah Parade. The man introduced himself as Mr Straples and said, welcome to the neighbourhood and told them that he owned the little shop. And he also asked how the boys intended to get the boat back up to Gordon Street. Peter, nor Anthony, could not answer that question and thought out loud that maybe their dad could come down and help them push it back.

Mr Straples said it might take more than one man and two boys to push it back up the hill and told them they could park it behind the gate, beside the shop if they wished, as it would be safe there and make it easier for them to use.

The boys thought it was a great idea and thanked Mr Straples, then pushed the boat over the road to the small beach beside the lake to rig up, ready for a sail.

It was a great place they thought for sailing but they did encounter shallow water until they got to almost past the jetty, this stopped them from inserting the keel into the water and made it just too difficult to sail, so they had to walk in the water, about thigh deep, and pull the boat to deep water, until they could push the keel all the way down.

They would get better at this Peter thought, and maybe learn to tack along the shoreline and move into deeper water gradually, plenty of time to learn.

The boys had a great time and packed up then pushed the boat over to the shop, opened the gate and parked the boat. Mr Straples came out of the shop and gave them the thumbs up, she'll be fine there fellows he said. What a great bloke, thought the boys as they walked up the hill to their home.

Mr Harris, arrived home from work that afternoon at about five pm, he was not very happy when he heard where the boat had been left and decided to check out this Mr Straples as it did not seem quite right, so he walked down the hill to the little shop on Tuggerah Parade.

Mr Straples was just taking in the 'Drink Coke' sign from the front of the shop as Mr Harris arrived at the shop, and said "Err, Mr Straples, is it"

"It is" answered Straples, "and what is it I can help you with, as you can see, I am just closing"

"I won't hold you up Mr Straples, my name is Harold Harris from just up on Gordon Street, behind you, and my boys tell me that their little boat is here."

Mr Straples, moved towards Mr Harris with his right arm outstretched, saying "Pleased to meet you Harold, I'm Jim" he replied, "Come on in and have a beer, Harold."

"Very nice of you Jim, sounds good" responded Mr Harris as he followed Jim Straples into the front of the shop. "Through here Harold," Jim called as he slid open a door behind the counter and entered a small room with a table and chairs amongst stock items for the shop, there was a fridge at the back of the room, next to a sink and cupboard, where Jim took two glasses from, then a bottle of Reshes Pilsener from the fridge and finally a small bottle opener that was sitting on the sink.

"Sit down Harold" Jim poured a beer into a glass and handed it to Harold, "they seem like nice kids, those boys of yours, Harold."

"Aye they're grandboys, ave they been a pest to ye tho," asked Harold.

"Not in the least, no, but I thought they were going to hurt themselves bringing that bloody boat down that hill today, just as well I was there to help, and I didn't want to see them trying to push the bugger back up there, cos I don't think it would have gone well, so I said they can leave it here if they want, plenty of room and I don't mind, I was a kid once too, you know."

"Bloody nice of yer Jim", Harold said, sipping his second beer, as Jim reached for another bottle in the fridge. "Where are you from Harold, Scotland?"

"Och no, not Scotland, Blackpool, south of Scotland, but I lived in Cumberland for a while and served with Lads from Scotland and the accent seems to stick a bit" Harold went on to mention Jack Higgins, "Fellow staying with us, Jack, is from Yorkshire and I have terrible trouble with his talking".

Jim, whilst getting the third bottle from the fridge, explained to Harold " I'm on my own down here, the wife died a few years and a bit ago, and I enjoy a bit of company now and again, so anytime Harold, Cheers!"

It was nearly seven o'clock when Mr Harris returned home and his dinner was in the oven, Mrs. Harris had insisted on eating dinner at 'dinner' time which was six pm, so too bad for Mr Harris, but, she thought, I hope he is alright!

Mrs Harris was a bit shocked when Mr Harris announced, whilst eating dinner alone, that he had invited Mr Straples for lunch, this coming Sunday, then added, if that's alright with you, of course.

It will have to be, I suppose, Mrs Harris, replied to the announcement.

Peter and Anthony, thought that was really good and they both thought Mr Straples to be a great bloke for helping them with the boat and letting them keep it at his shop.

On the following Sunday, after lunch, whilst Mr Harris and Mr Straples
were enjoying a beer, Mr Straples asked Peter if he had a prawn net, as the prawns were running because of the rain we were currently experiencing, but that it wouldn't last too much longer as the weather was starting to cool.

Peter replied that they do not have a prawn net, but that he had once been pawning on a boat at Buff Point. Mr Straples told Peter that hand prawning with a net was nothing like in a boat, he went on to say that he had one net and a pressure lamp and would show the boys how to catch prawns, if they were interested, and that he would buy any prawns they caught, if it was over six pounds in weight, as anything less would not be worthwhile to him, and he would cook them and sell them in his shop. That way they could then buy their own net, or nets and pressure lamps. What a great idea.

The next evening, as soon as it was dark, the whole family, including grandmother and Jack, were down at the lake in front of Mr Straples shop.

Mr Straples filled the lamp with methylated spirits, lit the wick, closed the top, then pumped the lamp up until it hurt the eyes to look at it.

"That's the way you want it" he said, raising the lamp high above his head, then picking up the prawn net with his other hand, headed into the lake, barefooted and wearing shorts, to about knee deep, everyone followed except for Mrs Harris and her mother.

Mr Straples pointed out, a little pair of red coloured eyes, then looking carefully you could see the outline of the prawn's body, looking long and rigid. Mr Straples said to be quiet, as noise scared them away, the he demonstrated how to catch a prawn, "you place the net, gently, behind the prawn, then place your foot, in front of the prawn. As he did this, the prawn simply jumped backwards into the prawn net. He then picked up a piece of seaweed that was floating nearby, broke off a small piece and placed it into the bottom of the net, he explained that this stopped the caught prawns from jumping out of the net. Wow, how easy is that?

He then passed the net to Peter and the lamp to Anthony and said that when the net is half full, then bring it over to the shop to empty, do not let the net become more than half full as the prawns will start to get out of the net, and also, the net will get too heavy, so, half full, empty out and back again for more, simple.

Then, Peter's dad, Jack and Mr Straples returned to Mr Straples's shop. Peter's mother and grandmother had, earlier returned to home.

It took the boys about four attempts, in about one and a half hours, with the net to get to just over six pounds of prawns. Mr Straples had said they were running quite good, and that they are not always this plentiful.

He paid the boys one and six a pound which equalled nine shillings, pretty good money for just over one hour's work.

School, the next day, so that was the end of the prawning, Peter and Anthony headed off leaving their dad and Uncle(as they were now calling him) Jack, behind with Mr Straples.

Things at school were good for all the children, it was now August 1961 and Peter would be going to high school next year, but there was not a high school at The Entrance, the nearest one being Gosford, nearly fifteen miles away, fortunately, there were school busses that ran from The Entrance to Gosford.

Things at Mr Harris's work were changing and Larry Kime had another project for the company's dredge in Sydney Harbour and had asked Mr Harris to take the dredge from Pitt Water to Birkenhead Point in Sydney and then to operate it there for about three months. Mr Harris was certainly keen as he had, had enough of the road construction he had been working on at, or near, Ourimbah.

Mr Harris, spoke with Mrs Harris about the new job and Mrs Harris was not too pleased, however, the more she thought about the prospect of living in Sydney, the more she warmed to it. She asked Mr Harris if there would be work for her mother's partner, Jack. Mr Harris said he would make it a condition for the dredge job, that Jack be given a job on the dredge. So that's how the Harris family had decided to move from Long Jetty to Sydney.

To find a house in Sydney was a little difficult, due to the distance for travel, so it was decided upon a home by looking in the Sydney newspapers only, and around where the dredge would be operating preferably. After much searching, finally, what sounded like, a suitable five bedroom home, with furniture, was found at Drummoyne, the only problem being that the amount of rent required was totally unaffordable, but there was really nothing else in the area available, Mrs Harris was also considering school locations and shopping.

On hearing about the high cost of rental properties in the area, Larry Kime offered to cover half of the rental costs for the Harris family for the duration of the Sydney dredging project.

Peter and Anthony, were devastated at the news of another move. Their protests were not ignored but rather talked around towards the betterment of being able to live in Sydney and very close to the city itself. They were also told, by their parents, that the school would be so much better than The Entrance school, to the response from the three children, was that they did not want to leave Long Jetty, full stop.

It was to no avail with respect to the children, they were under the control of their mother and father and they had to respect their parent's decisions.

The first hurtful part was for the boys having to sell their beloved VJ sailboat, fortunately, or unfortunately, depending on who was asked, the VJ sold almost instantly Peter mentioned selling around his school, with people putting their hands up everywhere. The boys also had at this stage, a small dog, that Anthony had bought from people from the last visiting circus in The Entrance, and although they were also told that the dog, would not be moving to Sydney, the boys performed to such a stage that the decision to leave the dog was reversed.

CHAPTER 11

Drummoyne

The Harris family, arrived at Day Street, Drummoyne in August 1961.

First look, as you arrived at the Day Street home, it was dingy looking with a very sad appearance from the front, it seemed to be a quite narrow looking building. But, upon opening the front door you then walked into a large vestibule with a double size staircase ascending to the next level, quite impressive really.

The rich dark red carpet with cream and green flourishes, followed the hallway which after some twenty five feet, turned to the left for about fifteen feet with yet another turn, now to the right with doors on both sides and extended all the way to the kitchen, which was almost the end of the house, with another door into the laundry, then a door to the outside of the house, revealing a very small backyard with a clothesline.

The laundry had a washing machine with a mangle placed on a swivel on the top of the machine, next to the machine were dual concrete tubs and sitting in the corner was a great cylindrical looking item, which was later discovered to be the hot water cistern, which was powered by gas.

The kitchen was complete with a six setting table and six chairs, a full length kitchen bench, with a window looking out to a brick wall of the house next door, in the middle of the bench, then another small bench leading up to a gas powered oven and cooktop, followed by two kitchen sinks, along the wall by the door that enters the hall, was another door that entered the pantry, within the pantry was also a door that entered the hallway. It was a huge kitchen. Along the hallway was a door that entered a toilet, a flushing toilet, and a basin. The last door in the hall went into a small office, or library, with an empty bookcase on one side and a desk and three chairs.

Along one wall in the kitchen were two doors, one led to the dining room with a table and eight chairs, a large sideboard occupied one end of the room whilst a large opening that led to the large lounge room, was to the other end. The other of the two doors leads to a smaller lounge with four lounge type chairs and ottomans and an open fireplace. There was also a door connecting to the larger lounge room.

The large lounge had a large open fireplace to the back wall with two three seater lounges, opposing each other on a right angle from the fireplace, there were also four lounge chairs, set in pairs toward the main pair of sliding glass panelled doors that led out to the vestibule.

The staircase went up to another hallway, with three bedrooms on the left hand side and two bedrooms and one bathroom on the right hand side.

Two of the bedrooms on the right had a double bed, an easy chair and a wardrobe, the other bedroom had two single beds with a desk in between the beds, a wardrobe and a single chair. Of the bedrooms on the other side, one had a double bed and a wardrobe and the other, had a single bed and a wardrobe.

Mrs Harris allocated the one single bed room to Marilyn and the room with the two single beds to the boys. Grandmother was to have the double bedroom next to the single bedroom, with Mr and Mrs Harris, the end double bedroom, leaving a spare double bedroom between the boy's room and the parent's room.

Peter's mother did not listen to any objections, the bedroom allocation was done!

No buts! We are going to the school to enrol all of you, even if it is only for three months. End of story! Was the answer given to all in response to "school? you are kidding, for three months? got to be joking."

Peter was certainly NOT looking forward to starting yet another school, four schools in two years, not good, unable to settle in. The other two children were in the same boat though, Peter supposed.

Drummoyne primary school, a short walk from Day Street was a pretty flash looking school, double story, red brick, it was similar to Blackpool primary school in looks, Peter thought as his mood changed slightly for the better.

It seemed very quiet and solemn, when the whole family, except the father, entered through the main entrance and into the administration area. The sound of a door closing in the distance seemed to echo and you could hear muffled voices, then a slightly raised voice, as in a comment. Our footsteps echoed up to the 'Information' desk. "Yes! Can I help you," the cheery lady asked.

"My name is Mrs Harris and these are my children whom I wish to enrol into this school".

"Please, take a seat, Mrs Harris, Mr Banning will be with you shortly".

After about ten minutes, the 'Information' lady called out. "He'll see you now Mrs Harris, just down the corridor, second door on your right!"

Hmm, very formal, thought Mrs Harris out loud, it's only a school, seems more like a hospital, as she escorted the children down the corridor.

The door was open and a bespectacled man could be seen sitting at a desk piled with files, he appeared to be busy writing, he did not look up, but having heard the footsteps come to a halt, called out, without looking up said: "Come right in, enrolment is it?, take a seat, the children can stand".

Peter, was of the opinion that he would not fit into this school very well, Anthony was also with that opinion, their little sister wouldn't know any different, they both assumed.

Mr Banning, was very brief, and issued Mrs Harris with some forms with the instruction to fill these out and have the children return them tomorrow morning at eight thirty, on the dot, at reception. "Good Morning".

And that was that none of the Harris's said a word until they emerged from the school, and then Mrs Harris commented, that it seems to be a very strict school and that it would do all good. Peter, certainly agreed about the strict bit and was not looking forward to school the next day.

The balance of that day was to the shopping centre and find a Fossey's store for new shoes and shorts for both boys and school dress for Marilyn.

Mrs Harris, took them into Woolworths first for lunch at the cafeteria, wow thought Peter, this place is just like Blackpool as they all looked at the menu. Peter already knew what he wanted as soon as he saw it being served to someone at the server, Mrs Harris asked Marilyn what she wanted, then asked Anthony, and said "Braised steak and mashed potatoes for you, I suppose" looking at Peter, she knew it was his favourite food.

Peter tried to stop thinking about school tomorrow.

The Day Street house, made a very comfortable home and Mrs Harris was over the moon with it, no more outside visits for the toilet here, she thought, and flushing toilets too, and a lovely shower over the bath. Just everything about it was good, and the room, she had to go into the lounge to see if the kids were still there as she could not hear them. Her mother just loved the kitchen and was already baking pies and cakes, just lovely. No more dirt and dust, flies and smells and saying smells her mind went back to Buff Point with the long drop and the smell..uggh, but Long Jetty with the toilet bins was even a worse smell than the long drop.

The Drummoyne school was nothing like any of the previous schools that Peter had attended since living in Australia, this, he thought was definitely like England except for the hot meals. Everyone at Drummoyne primary seemed to wear a school uniform, unlike the country, or bush, schools he'd been to where barefoot was the norm.

It did not take long to make friends in his class and his new teacher, Mr Donald, seemed to be very young for a teacher, he was always talking about the Australian bush and camping, shooting kangaroos, shooting foxes, shooting dingoes. He certainly seemed to like shooting. He was very keen to hear about Peter's previous schools and very interested about Peter's VJ sailboat, as he was also a keen sailor and just loved sailing his 'Flying Fifteen' on 'The Harbour", when he was not away shooting.

Mr Donald, was also a keen Rugby Union player and for sport, every Friday he took the Drummoyne Primary School Junior Rugby Union team for training, and if you are in his class and you are a boy, then you are in his team, Peter was told by others in the class. Peter really like playing union with Mr Donald's team as he moved you around into different positions.

Being the last semester at primary school for the sixth grade students, concentration was on key subjects that would be encountered in high school next year. At this stage all the sixth grade kids were quite excellent with their time's tables, well, thought Peter, most, so maths with money was a big issue and so were weights and distances. Certainly not Peter's domain as none of it really made sense to him. Why, do twelve pennies make one shilling, but twenty shillings make one pound?

Peter remembered an American friend, called Pat, that his father had in England who visited them on occasions with his German wife Erica.

Peter remembered him saying to his father that he could not handle the 'Mickey Mouse' money in England and that it was a completely broken system and quoted that in the States, it takes ten cents, a cent being like a penny, to make a dime, a dime being like a shilling, then ten dimes to make a dollar, a dollar being like a pound. Makes far better sense he said, and much easier to calculate with.

Wow, thought Peter, how easy would school be if ten pennies made one shilling and ten shillings made one pound? Pat's wife, Erica, said the same thing when buying food, England is sixteen ounces to a pound of food, in Germany, it all works in tens, such as one hundred grams to one kilo, or for liquids, rather than have eight pints to a gallon, they have one hundred millilitres to a litre. Much simpler. If only!

During a school, math lesson, where Peter was struggling with his calculations and his mind running wild with his thoughts of Pat and Erica, not to mention that Mr Donald, was a nice and amicable teacher, he considered putting a question to his teacher in respect to the difference between these countries and their currency systems, so, he put his hand up, "Yes, Mr Harris"

"Sir, beg your pardon Sir", Peter nervously started, "why is it that in America, Sir, that they have only ten cents, a cent being like a penny, to make a nickel, a nickel like a shilling, and ten nickels to make a dollar, a dollar being like a pound, Sir"

Mr Donald, quick as a flash replied, "Because", young Mr Harris, "the Americans are very bad at maths". The class erupted with laughter, Peter, felt silly.

Mr Donald, followed to the class with a loud "I AM ONLY JOKING, SETTLE DOWN"

And went on, "Very, very good question Harris. Indeed, it is indeed a much simpler system, and I am not sure where the American adoption actually came from. We here, in Australia, inherited, our monetary system from the British Imperial system, whereas, in the old days items were traded and copper wire was a favourite, in England as it was rich in copper. The imperial penny was actually divided into four, the smallest being known as a farthing being one of nine hundred and sixty parts of one pound sterling. So copper was weighed out as such, for example, a chicken may have been sold for one shilling which would relate to forty eight pieces of the copper wire known as a farthing. In order to abbreviate this to make it easier, a half penny became two farthings and a penny became four farthings and twelve of these pennies became 48 farthings which equalled one shilling sterling. Shillings in sterling became the imperial British currency"

Mr Donald went on to say "It is not only our currency that Australia has adopted but also weights and measures wish are also based on a similar scale as the currency. But!, let me tell you that moves are afoot to change all of our present, adopted, systems to a more sensible, metric, system of measurement, and that may happen within the next few years, hopefully". Mr Donald then concluded with, "BUT!, it is not here yet, so we are using the imperial system, so heads down and do your best".

After the school bell had rang and the class was leaving for the day, Mr Donald approached Peter and told him how much he had enjoyed receiving such a question and that the present imperial system, was not only his, pet hate, but also many teachers in NSW, and that various actions and petitions are presently being presented to the Federal Parliament, for Australia to go metric.

Peter felt quite proud of himself for asking that question in class, and a couple of the other students thought it was a good question also, as it had broken the boredom of a maths lesson.

December was approaching, and Larry Kime's company had not yet received notification of a new contract in Sydney Harbour. In fact there were but a few weeks only remaining on the present contract.

Wellington

Mr and Mrs Harris were having, what was now seeming to be, a regular discussion, on where to move to for Mr Harris's employment, and Mrs Harris did not enjoy these conversations. Larry Kime had told Mr Harris, that without the contract he was expecting, then at this point, he had no work for the tug or the dredge. He did, however, have work for Mr Harris, back on the road construction near Gosford, or at the new Vales Point Power Station.

Mrs Harris was of the belief, that were only going backwards if they returned to The Entrance area. She was also of the belief, that working for Kime was always going to involve moving house and that she had, had enough of moving, especially so much of it over such a short time. She also said that it was not fair on the children, especially moving school all the time, and her mother was also becoming fed up with moving.

Mr Harris, needed to look for some type of regular, long term employment which would allow the family to settle down. Sadly, what Mr Harris required, didn't seem to be available for him at this stage.

There was not really the type of work that Mr Harris was compatible with, other than working on the ferries around Sydney, he wasn't too keen on that, plus the ferry wage would not allow them to keep renting this home in Drummoyne.

Mr Harris had been told of work on the Burrendong Dam that may be up to five years work, as it was due to be completed in 1967, that could mean up to five years work for him.

Mr and Mrs Harris, together with Mrs Harris's mother and Jack Higgins, decided to give the Burrendong Dam a try.

Mr Harris sold his 1954 Holden sedan to Jack Higgins and bought a 1960 model Peugeot 403 station wagon, which had much more room than the Holden.

It was early December 1961 when the Harris's, and the Higgins, were packed and ready for the two hundred and thirty mile trip to Wellington NSW, being the closest town to the Burrendong Dam project.

The journey to Wellington took the families west of Sydney towards the Blue Mountains, everyone was in awe at the sights, and scenic views were stopped quite regularly and involuntarily, in a couple of incidents when the Holden overheated and boiled. Mr Harris had a quiet conversation with Jack Higgins in respect to using a lower gear, like second gear, rather than third gear so much and that this will cause the car's engine fan to work more efficiently.

This seemed to be very effective and the Holden did not boil again during the journey.

They had travelled only sixty five miles when at four thirty that afternoon, found them at the top of the mountains at The Hydro Majestic hotel, just before Medlow Bath. Mrs Harris thought it may be a bit of good therapy for everyone if they all stayed here for the night and enjoyed a special dinner because they didn't really know where they would be tomorrow night. There were no objections.

What a lovely Hotel, Mrs Harris and Jack Higgins went to the reception and checked into three rooms, the cost was certainly much more than she had imagined but had decided it would make it up to the children a little for leaving Drummoyne.

That evening they all dined at the incredible restaurant that had a majestic view over the Megalong Valley. Peter thought it resembled the Orontes dining room the way the settings were laid out and the menu. Peter had already found the history of the hotel and enlightened everyone whilst waiting for their meals, and when Peter mentioned Mark Foy, his mother lifted her head, as she had been shopping in Mark Foy's in Sydney, only a week ago, a very impressive hotel.

They did not have breakfast the next morning at the Majestic, Peter could not understand why, as the dinner had been superb, when he asked his mother why, she just brushed it aside and said that all would be having breakfast a little later, down the road.

The breakfast stop was to be Lithgow, about twenty six miles from the hotel they had stayed at.

Following breakfast, it was pleasant, though somewhat a hot drive of eighty miles to Mudgee for a toilet stop and a break, then through to Wellington a further sixty miles, arriving around lunchtime.

The first thing everyone noticed upon arrival at Wellington was the heat. Jack Higgins, whilst buying cold drinks for everyone at the Cow and Calf Hotel's beer garden, had learned that the temperature was one hundred point nine degrees Fahrenheit. But it was lovely in the beer garden sipping on a cold drink and the lunch was great.

Following lunch, it seemed to Mr and Mrs Harris, in conjunction with the Higgins family, that the Cow and Calf may be the place to stay until more information has been gathered with respect to employment at the Burrendong Dam site, then a more permanent type of accommodation may be sought.

It didn't take Peter and Anthony very long to find the Wellington public swimming pool that was directly across the road from the Cow and Calf Hotel.

The family was to be staying here for at least a week, Peter and Anthony thought that was unreal, could not be better.

Mr Harris and Jack Higgins, both found work at the Burrendong Dam construction site. The only more permanent accommodation for the families seemed to be the caravan park beside the Macquarie River, a thirty minute walk into town. There were many houses for rent around Wellington but none that were furnished, and Mrs Harris was not going to buy furniture for a house in Wellington, because she did not think she would be here, in Wellington for a very lengthy time as she found the heat, the dust, the flies and the facilities in Wellington oppressive. Peter and Anthony, thought it was a great town.

The children found the caravan park very hard to live in after living in the 'mansion' at Drummoyne. Mrs Harris was not very happy either and was thinking that if they were to get a home here and buy furniture, then what was Mr Harris going to do for work once the dam was finished? It was not, going to happen.

The children had not been enrolled into school at Wellington as it was only a couple of weeks to the school holidays when they had arrived in Wellington.

See how things are looking in January thought Mrs Harris.

Both the boys spent almost every day walking the thirty minutes from the caravan park to the swimming pool in the morning and returning late in the afternoon. It was really good at the pool, though it was very quiet and they had the run of the complex, until three thirty each afternoon when school was finished, then it became very busy and time for the boys to leave.

The walk to the pool took the boys past the Wellington Cordial Factory and after a few times of walking past, a worker called out to them, "it's hot boys, do yous want a drink?" They could not resist and the lady took them inside the factory and showed them a fridge and told them to help themselves, they certainly did and thanked the lady, who said anytime you are walking past call in.

The days just dragged on in Wellington, Mr Harris and Jack Higgins worked about ten hours a day and seven days a week. They said it was fantastic money and Mrs Harris said, for what! A life here, living in a caravan, sweating all day long and can't cool down. Peter's mum, was not happy and it affected the children.

Christmas 1961, came and went, a week later it was 1962.

Christmas was enjoyed by both families as they made the best of it as they could, Peter got a Stirling .22 single shot rifle for Christmas and Anthony got a Dianne .177 air rifle.

Peter could not remember what his sister got for Christmas, a doll he thought, most likely.

Peter had been taught about rifles, when going to work with his father on occasions, at Ourimbah, by the foreman on the job named Tom, who was also a local ranger around that area. Tom had been meticulous with respect to safety and respect with firearms also whilst teaching Peter, Peter had enjoyed shooting with Tom.

Peter went shooting with his father and Anthony with the caravan park manager who also owned the property around the caravan park. It was really good except Mr Harris was using Peter's rifle and Peter was just watching, but his father said he would get a turn later. Rabbits seemed to be everywhere, but they also seemed to be very quick, too quick, it seemed for Peter's father.

At the end of the day, they had five rabbits, the park manager shot four and Peter shot one. As the Harris family did not have an oven in the caravan, the manager took all the rabbits home with him but invited the Harris family, and the Higgins for dinner that evening. What a great meal and night everyone had.

By the end of January 1962, both Mrs Harris and her mother had seen enough of living in a caravan in Wellington, it was just too hot, too far to walk to town and just, too much.

A decision had to be made, Wellington was a nice town, with nice people, but, living in a caravan next to the river, was not nice.

With only about four years of dam work remaining, was it worth getting a home and staying, or moving on to something more substantial? Moving on, seemed to be the general consensus.

Mr Harris and Jack Higgins had both heard, at the Burrendong Dam site, that there was heaps happening down at 'the snowy', where the conditions were good and unbelievable pay.

It took little to convince Mrs Harris that 'the snowy' was to be the family's destination.

A course was set for Cooma, where the Snowy Mountains Authority headquarters were located. Some three hundred miles south.

The first day of travel stopped at Yass, with both families staying at the Australian Hotel - Motel for the evening, six hours on the road in temperatures of over 100°F was enough. While Peter's parents relaxed with drinks at the hotel, Peter and Anthony walked to the Yass Memorial Swimming Pool, which they had passed on the way to the hotel, it was just over a half mile walk and well worth the walk to jump into the cool water after travelling on those dusty roads from Wellington.

Dinner that evening was at the hotel dining room, following dinner Mr Harris and Jack Higgins walked through the rear carpark of the motel part of the hotel, where we were staying, through to the Yass Soldiers Club.

Mrs Harris took the children to the Liberty Theatre, which was located just across the road, on the main street from the hotel, to watch the latest released movie 'The Sundowners'. What a great movie, thought Peter, but it made him think of his family travelling all the time, just like the movie.

Following breakfast at the hotel's dining room, it was time to head to Cooma, one hundred and twenty miles south.

Everyone settled down to another hot days travel, except now it was a bitumen roadway, no more dirt.

The route to Cooma went through Canberra and the first Canberra suburb of Lyneham was seen just before lunchtime, it was a very new suburb being commenced in only 1958, a year before the Harris's had landed in Australia.

The road veered to the right at Lyneham and the road turned into the Federal Highway and then just where the suburb of Ainslie started the road became Canberra Avenue. They approached a large pine plantation and a sign saying Braddon, here they turned to the left with the vision of a Caltex sign to fuel the cars.

Having fuelled, then finding Coggan's Bakery just down the road from the Caltex, lunch was had of meat pies, sausage rolls and pasties.

According to the recently bought road map, it was then back on to turning left onto Canberra Avenue and continuing all the way through to the Cooma Road which should be to the right after approximately five miles. Easy as.

Driving through the city, they just bypassed the main 'Civic' shopping centre, according to the road signs, around a large hill and then down onto a huge bridge called Commonwealth Avenue Bridge, but there was no water under it, just a small river, the Molonglo River. To the left of this bridge, in the distance was another huge bridge, which seemed to span the same small river, a large building was under construction to to left towards the end of this Commonwealth Avenue Bridge.

A bit further along to the right was the Albert Hall, and large white coloured buildings with red roofs to the left with a sign 'Administration Buildings'

The traffic was very light compared to what they were used to in Sydney, but it was around here they seemed to have become lost.

Just past a sign 'Capitol Hill Hostel' both cars turned left onto Sydney Avenue and arrived at Telopia Park High School.

After much map consultation, and a little blue language, it was discovered that Dominion Circuit should take them back to Canberra Avenue, which it did, after that it was past a place, another shopping centre, called Manuka, and then finally a sign to the right for Monaro Highway, Cooma.

It had taken an unbelievable two and a half hours since they had driven past Lyneham to get to the Cooma turnoff, it was now about one thirty in the afternoon with about one and a half hours time until Cooma some sixty five miles distance.

The sign said Bredbo and the little pub with people sitting at tables outside looked too inviting for Mr Harris as he suggested to Mrs Harris that a cool drink could be the order of the day, to which Mrs Harris instantly agreed with just enough time to turn abruptly to the right into the hotel's small car park.

Jack Higgins, following in the Holden did not, however, have time to see the place to turn off and proceeded along the highway to Cosgrove Street and turned around there to come back to the hotel.

Mr Harris called out to Jack Higgins as he stopped the Holden, that by the time they get into Cooma, the day will be done, so they might as well take it easy.

Drinks were enjoyed at the front of the Bredbo Hotel.

Mrs Harris had struck up a conversation with a lady who was travelling from Cooma to Queanbeyan, having lived for a year or so in Cooma, whilst her husband was at a SMHEA work camp near Khancoban, her husband explained that SMHEA was the Snowy Mountains Hydro Electricity Authority.

He added that the main employer was Thiess Brothers who had over forty thousand people employed, and the SMHEA around sixty thousand. He also said the work was dangerous and that there had been about 120 deaths on the project.

It seemed that Mrs Harris was already losing interest in Cooma.

They stayed at the Royal Hotel in Cooma, it was just past the busy part of the town on the corner of Lambie and Sharp Streets. It was also a motel type of accommodation, similar to that at Yass, the previous night.

Mr Harris and Jack Higgins had plans to visit the SMHEA employment office the next morning.

That afternoon, we walked through the main street of Cooma, down one side and back to the hotel on the other, where they came across the Southern Cloud Memorial.

They learnt that the Southern Cloud, was a passenger aeroplane that had crashed in the rugged snowy mountain ranges near Tooma, in 1931 carrying eight passengers and two crew. The airplane had been lost, undiscovered, until 1958, some twenty seven years later. It may never have been found except for the Snowy Mountain Hydro project workers in

1958 when building access roads to the Deep Creek access tunnel, for the hydro system.

Dinner that night at the hotel, this was becoming a very enjoyable habit Peter thought. Early night for all, early rising and breakfast at the hotel, then off to the SMHEA offices just north of town

Peter, of course, had no knowledge of the meeting that had taken place in the hotel bar last night, with Mr and Mrs Harris and Mrs Harris's mother and Jack Higgins.

Following Mrs Harris's conversation earlier that day with the people they had met at Bredbo, Mrs Harris, had been doing a little research in town that afternoon with respect to the danger of working on the Snowy scheme, the accommodation and school facilities in the camps and the housing, accommodation available in Cooma.

The results of Mrs Harris's research, though very brief, were not good on all fronts.

The work available, if any, for both Mr Harris and Mr Higgins would, it seemed, most likely require them to be accommodated in a work camp, which she did not want that Mr Harris would be away from his family, which was one of the main reasons for migrating to Australia.

The accommodations at the camps that permitted families were few in number and mostly unstable for children.

The accommodation in and around Cooma was very sparse, from what she had been told. But, the main factor of her concern was the danger that also seemed to be involved.

It was true that almost one hundred men had been killed on this project since its launch in 1949. There were many more deaths in relation to the project. These included transport accidents when delivering equipment and materials for the project, unloading materials and equipment and many more instances.

The number of fatalities did not include near fatalities or mutilations causing severe hardship. It also did not include accidents that caused injuries so severe that some men could never work again, and that some were crippled for life. And some died many years after, following complications from injuries received on the project which were never attributed to the death count as per the current period of time.

The bottom line was, Mrs Harris did not want Mr Harris to work on the Snowy Mountains Project. It was decided to go to Queanbeyan NSW.

The Harris and the Higgins families arrived at the Donald Road caravan park at about lunchtime after driving the sixty six miles from Cooma.

Two, site rental, caravans were available, one with a large awning containing two single beds in addition to a double and two single beds in the caravan

CHAPTER 12

Queanbeyan

Mrs Harris's mother had decided to return to England as she thought it was just a bit too rough for her liking, and certainly too much travelling for her and Jack Higgins. They had booked a passage on the ship Himalaya and left for Sydney by train from the Canberra Railway Station. They had barely been in Australia for two years.

Mr and Mrs Harris took Mrs Harris's mother and Jack Higgins to the Canberra Railway Station and said their goodbyes.

Meanwhile, in Queanbeyan, Anthony and Marilyn were enrolled at the Queanbeyan primary school on Isabella Street and could travel by bus from Anne Street, which was the last street to intersect with Donald Road, from there south was all bushland, which the boys had already explored and had been there shooting.

Peter, chose to walk to the High school on Agnes Avenue, a twenty minute walk of about a mile.

Peter loved high school and thought it was really good, different, but good, and it was easy to make new friends. The people that ran the caravan park, were the Donnelly family, comprising of Mr and Mrs Donnelly, their eldest son Peter, who had just left high school and was now seeking a job with a career, Tim Donnelly, who was about a year older than Peter, who would often dink Peter to school on his bike, then the youngest of the family, Michael, who was at primary school with Anthony and Marilyn, they shared the same school bus and all became good friends.

Mr Harris found a job at the Australian Blue Metal quarry as a diesel fitter, a trade he had been taught as part of his MED2 in the merchant navy.

The quarry was located on the Federal Highway eighteen miles from the caravan park at Queanbeyan.

Mrs Harris was concerned about the distance Mr Harris had to travel, but Mr Harris, told her it was fine, he liked the job and, that there may be a chance of promotion, as the loader driver had been taken sick and they were trying to find a driver, when Mr Harris told the quarry manager, that he had recently been operating a similar Michigan front end loader during road construction works, so he was now, the fill in.

About a week after driving the loader at the quarry, it was discovered that the loader driver would not be returning to work due to a medical condition and Mr Harris was asked if he would like the position as loader driver. It was also explained to Mr Harris that a substantial pay increase came with the job.

Mr Harris was over the moon, but then, unbelievably, the manager went on to say that a company on site house also came with that position, as on occasions there may be urgent loadings to be done during the evenings or weekends.

These loading were classified as urgent for the reason, that, Australian Blue Metal has a contract with the SMHEA in Cooma for the supply of road base and other blue metal products to their sites around the Snowy project, these sites are around one hundred and fifty miles, some times further, from the quarry. The trucks are loaded the night before for departure the next morning and it is, generally, a five hour drive to the site and a four hour drive back to the quarry. As a rule, the trucks should be back, empty at the quarry by around four o'clock in the afternoon, but, due to adverse road conditions and sometimes, breakdowns, these trucks may be late getting back, but they still require loading regardless of the time. So, hence the house is supplied free of charge for the loader driver.

Mr Harris accepted the job in a drawn out sort of, "Gee's Jim, I'll have to talk to the wife about it". When in fact, Mr Harris was over the moon.

The quarry manager added, "Well, if you will take it 'Harry', then I'll chuck in a company ute and petrol, the other bloke didn't get that"

Mr Harris was not really expecting that and said, "Sounds good to me, the wife will just have to like it".

Mr Harris could hardly wait to get home that afternoon to tell Mrs Harris and the children about their good fortune. He had only been at the quarry for three months and he landed the second best job at the quarry, more money, a house and a utility that he could use for his own personal use. You bloody ripper.

Mrs Harris and the children were so excited about the prospect of living out at the quarry, but they became a little less excited when they were told that they could not go to look at it until the former loader driver had vacated the house. The quarry company had given the former driver one month to vacate, or longer if he needed it. His name was Robbo, and he seemed to Mr Harris to be a decent sort of fellow.

Peter and Anthony were very excited about the new move and asked their father heaps of questions about, how much land is there, what the house was like, how many people lived there, can we go shooting there. They went on and on, but to no avail, as their father did not know the answers at this stage.

Sutton

It was the following Monday afternoon when Mr Harris arrived home from work at the quarry and announced that, Robbo, had moved out of the house over the weekend, and that he just needed a couple of days to give it a good cleanout. And then it's ours. The loud HURRAH from the children made him jump, he was not expecting that. He went on to say that he and Mrs Harris needed to get some furniture together and to get it delivered out there, before the weekend on Thursday and Friday, especially beds, so that we can move in on the Saturday.

The following day Mrs Harris went furniture shopping at T E Woodger & Sons, in Monaro Street, Queanbeyan. At their auction rooms, she found a double and three second hand beds, with new mattresses, or almost, together with a kitchen table and six chairs, and another Silent Knight refrigerator, that was in excellent condition. They were unable to deliver these items until the Saturday morning, if that would suit madam, they said. Mrs Harris was sure Saturday would be perfect. She then went further down Monaro Street to J B Young's, where she bought new sheets and some more blankets.

Mr Harris told Peter that he found out the nearest school bus was at the NSW - ACT border, which is about three quarters of a mile from the house, but the school bus does not go to Queanbeyan, only to Canberra Suburbs.

Sadly for Peter, looks like a new high school, there was however a primary school at Sutton, so they will have to check out the school situation after they moved into their new house. Pretty exciting, but a bit sad, meaning new schools, again!

Saturday morning, finally, arrived, there was not very much of the Harris's possessions to take, as Mr Harris had been taking things every day on his way to work. The boys, push bikes, had been taken along with various items so that all that was remaining was their clothing, pillows, sheets and blankets and crockery and cutlery. It seemed to take Mrs Harris, hours just to check that we had not left anything behind in the caravan, as the children waited, impatiently, in the Peugeot station wagon.

The house was amazing, it was a very neat farmhouse, with three bedrooms, and an 'L' shaped lounge of which part of was a dining room. There was a very large kitchen with a breakfast bar. There was a bathroom inside the house, but the laundry and toilet were outside, and yes,...another toilet with a can,....no!

Mrs Harris was thrilled, even though they had another dry toilet, as they called them. The boys spent all of thirty seconds inside the house, then were out the door exploring.

There was another, slightly smaller looking, farmhouse type of home, about one hundred and fifty yards from their house, this, Mr Harris had told them, was probably the farm workers' cottage, back in its day, it was now occupied by the Quarries vehicle service foreman, who lived on site to organise any breakdowns, and that he, himself would work on vehicles during the night, or weekends if needed.

To the north, there were two sheds about fifty yards from their house and then, what looked like about a mile away were three other buildings. About sixty yards in from of the house, was the dirt road that led up to the quarry, about five hundred yards up the road and well before the quarry, on left hand side of the road, was the weighbridge and the fuel bowsers, on the right hand side stood a huge workshop. The road went on another five hundred or so yards to the crushing plant and then wound up the hill, about another seven hundred or more yards to the quarry benches. To the southeast, of their house, you could see the stockpile of quarry products that seemed to go on for miles.

The next day, Sunday, when the quarry was not working, Mr Harris took the family for a tour of their surroundings in the company's Holden Utility.

Of course, Peter and Anthony had to sit in the back with the rest of the family in the front bench seat of the ute.

Firstly up and onto the weighbridge, passing six Foden bogey drive tip trucks, then to the bowser to fill the ute with petrol. It was then to the left to drive in front of the huge workshop.

It was an open workshop with five huge bays, two gigantic Foden dump trucks were in a bay each, one with its wheels off, and one with its body slightly raised. Another building next to the workshops was a staff amenities shed, then up past the crushing plant's array of storage bins and conveyor belts, following a very windy road that led to four roads leading from the road we were on.

Mr Harris explained that the roads went to different quarry levels and that this was as far as we could safely go into the quarry.

Going back down the hill and past everything that we saw on the way up, as we approached our house, and going past it to another road to the right, Mr Harris, turned here and kept going, the road got rougher, all the way, about a mile and a bit, to the shearing shed. Mr Harris explained that all this land on their side of McLaughlins Creek was part of the quarry companies lease, including the shearing shed, shearers quarters, shed kitchen and amenities shed, and sheep yards. All were quite amazed and really looking forward to living here.

Mr Harris then drove back to their house, then right, onto the quarry road up to the front gate which was locked, passing a key through the window of the ute to Peter sitting on the back. Peter, jumped from the ute, opened the gate, waited for the family to drive through, locked the gate and jumped back onto the ute.

Mr Harris turned right onto the Federal Highway and drove the one mile to the border, then at a sign saying, Majura Lane, which was a dirt road, he turned left into the lane and stopped in front of the hugest tree any of the Harris family had ever seen. It was so big, with smooth, pale brown and dark brown bark, its branches reached well over to the other side of the road and initials could be seen, etched into the bark of the tree.

"That is the school bus stop," Mr Harris said to Peter, "and on the other side of the road, is still part of the quarry lease, all the way to the ACT-NSW border"

They then drove into Sutton Village and went past the primary school to their right, then just as the road turned very sharply to the left, then to the right was the Sutton General store, which just happened to be closed.

Just on five mile, said Mr Harris, "but there is no school bus from where we are" he said to Mrs Harris, "You might need to learn to drive Mary!"

The owner of all the land under lease by the quarry, Bevan Carmody, just lived seven blocks up from the shop. Mr Harris had met

Mr Carmody at the shearing shed. He told Mr Harris, that he had it in the lease, to use the shed once a year, but, other than that, it was the quarry's to use, for its designed purpose only, of course, as with the quarters and the kitchen. It was a big lease of just over nine hundred acres, the reason so big, was for flying rocks being a danger for any workers and stock around the quarry area when blasting face rock, and room for an airfield, for the O'Neils, which was already in place and used on occasions.

The airstrip had also been handy for crop dusting operations for the local graziers.

Mrs Harris had put, 'learn to drive' at the top of her list, as they headed back to their new house for the second night. What an adventure this is going to be thought Peter.

Monday morning, Mr Harris had taken some time off work later that morning, when things were quiet, all the company trucks were out as with most of the subcontractors. This time taken was to drive Mrs Harris together with Anthony and Marilyn to the Sutton primary school for enrolment there.

Mrs Harris, thought it was marvellous, however, she was informed that Sutton Primary School could not cater for Anthony as they did not teach past year three primary.

It was then decided that, as Anthony would be attending Lyneham primary school, Marilyn may well also attend Lyneham primary school as Anthony could look after her, coming and going to school, as by the time Anthony moved to high school next year, then she, Mrs Harris, will be able to drive Marilyn to primary school.

The next day, Mr Harris, again took some time from work to take the family to Lyneham Primary and Lyneham High School for school enrolments.

Everything was just going perfectly for all the Harris's. Christmas 1962 was upon them before they knew it and they enjoyed their fourth Christmas in Australia.

The best thing was, they were all thinking, no more moves in the near future as Mr Harris enjoyed his work and the quarry had at least another ten years supply of materials.

It was now mid 1963, lots had happened, Mr Harris had bought lambs from a neighbouring property, with the view of fattening them for about a year.

Peter, had a weekend job at a poultry farm at Pialligo, although it was nine miles from home, he was able to get a lift from another weekend worker who travelled from Gundaroo to the poultry farm and would pick Peter up from the main gate.

Peter's workmate from Gundaroo was Bob Bevan, who worked on a station during the week, and, as weekends were boring out there, he chose to work at the poultry farm on weekends, where he said, he earned nearly as much in two days, as what he earned at Gundaroo in a week.

Bob, was the 'feed batcher' at the farm, as the farm was a force laying farm, meaning that the hens lay two eggs each day, through controlled light. Bob would make up a batch of mixed, balanced protein food, with vitamins and steroids into a five ton hopper each day, as the hens were fed twice a day.

Peter, who started as a feeder, three months prior, had advanced to the frozen chicken preparation room, which was one of the better paid jobs on the farm.

Mr Harris had bought a new car, just before last Christmas, an EJ Holden for £2,660.00, it was a Holden Special, and Mr Harris had been teaching Peter's mother how to drive, but to no avail. She was good at steering, reverse parking, parking at the curb between two cars, and knew all the rules of the road explicitly.

She just could not change gears whilst driving. She would lose concentration on the road when changing gear, as she felt she had to look down at her left foot and her left hand when she changed gear. This would cause her to veer to the left to the extent of driving off the road.

Jim, the quarry manager, had just been given a new company car which was also an EJ Holden, but it was a 1963 model EJ, rather than Mr Harris's 1962 model EJ.

The biggest difference between these two Holden cars, which looked identical, even their colours of grey with a white roof, but Jim's car was called a Hydromatic.

Which meant automatic transmission.

Jim was aware of Mrs Harris's driving issue and suggested to Mr Harris to take his wife for a driving lesson in his automatic Holden, to see how she goes with it.

Mr Harris did this and the result was nothing short of amazing, she had not a worry in the world when driving Jim's automatic car.

Mr Harris, told Jim about the difference in Mrs Harris's driving and suggested to Jim that they swap cars. Jim declined the kind offer but said his boss would find out and they would both be looking for jobs. Mr Harris admitted he was only joking and asked Jim for some time off the next day, to trade his new Holden for an automatic.

Mr and Mrs Harris drove into Canberra the next morning, they went to where Mrs Harris had bought their car from, Beazley and Bruce, about about eight months earlier.

The salesman at Beazley and Bruce, listened to what Mr and Mrs Harris said they would like, but sadly they had no automatics sedans in stock, other than a Premier model EJ Holden. The premier model car also had a premier price tag at £4,400.00, but they would trade Mr Harris's car in at a good price of £1,900,00.

Mr Harris, told the salesman, in no uncertain, terms that he was not going to lose £760 in such a short period, and that they would go and check out the new Valiant cars that had just been introduced into Australia.

The salesman at Beazley and Bruce suggested that Mr and Mrs Harris, take the premier model Holden for a drive, while he would speak with his manager.

Once the Harris's drove the premier model Holden, they were sold, it was nothing like their standard, special model Holden. This one had leather bucket seats in the front, a heater with a three speed fan, and a car radio.

They had decided to buy the premier even before they had returned to the dealership. The salesman greeted them with a surprise revaluation of their Holden to £2,100.00. the Harris's agreed.

As the quarry, where they lived was in NSW, Mrs Harris had to go to Queanbeyan for her license test which she passed on her first appointment.

Mr Harris was earning good money working at the quarry and living rent free.

It was about this time that a huge company called Readymix, bought out ABM.

Things didn't change much for Mr Harris except he had to pay rent for the house, but in return, he got paid overtime when loading the trucks after hours. They also told Mr Harris, he could have as many sheep as he wanted in the paddocks around the quarry, but they would not guarantee their safety from missiles from the quarry.

There was a work camp at the quarry consisting of six dongers and an amenities block with a separate kitchen. These were located on the right side of the road heading to the airfield. It was generally occupied by the jackhammer operators on the quarry floor, these were very itinerant workers. One other worker who occupied a donger was a man called Ernie, who worked as a greaser on the crusher plant. Ernie, also worked as the cook when the shearers were at the quarry each year, he seemed to enjoy starting early at the shearing camp before work at the quarry, then working a short shift at the quarry, and then returning to the shearing camp at around three o clock in the afternoon, to prepare dinner. It worked well for him as he got paid a very good wage for the cooking, plus he had his meals with the shearers.

Mr Harris found out that Ernie was also a butcher. Ernie had asked Mr Harris for a price on fat lambs, for meat for the shearers. This was a short, but very good market for Mr Harris's lambs. It did later extend from the shearer's meat supply to the quarry workers' meat supply also, thanks to Ernie, for the price of a half carton of Reshes Dinner Ale, plus a side of lamb, to butcher three sheep.

Peter had been bringing home some 'unsexed' day or two old chicks from the farm he worked at, these were given to Peter, rather than be destroyed, as when they obtain the day old chicks in cartons, they need to sex them, keep the pullets (females), and reject the males, (cocks). This is done by a specialist known as a 'sexer', but, there are some chicks that the sexer, due to the speed required in sexing the chicks, can not determine the sex, these are put aside and either, re sexed in a few weeks, or discarded.

Peter had set up incubators in one of the big sheds near the house, the incubators were made from old arc lights that were discarded from the quarry and Peter fitted them with one hundred and twenty watt clear globes. He had made up three half circular shaped areas in three corners of the shed, using empty five gallon drums, that were in abundance at the quarry dump. These were filled with blue metal dust, called 'cracker dust' which was also in abundance, then discarded, jackhammer rods, also from the quarry dump, were placed in these drums.

Wire netting, which he also found around the quarry, was attached to the sticks, to create three enclosures.

All the day, or two day chicks went into one enclosure with an incubator, until their combs told of which sex they were. Peter, then separated the pullets to another enclosure, with an incubator, and the cocks to the last enclosure and incubator.

As the pullets got bigger, to the point of laying they were put out in the main shed to run free and use the laying boxes in a row against one wall. The cocks were retained in their enclosure and Peter sold these as fresh chickens to the quarry workers and truck drivers, as with the eggs.

Sadly, Peter could not freeze these chickens or he would have made a fortune.

But, they were soon, becoming too much for him to handle, feeding and watering in the mornings before and after school. And it stunk in that shed, hens were also getting out and making a mess around the house, which, both his mother and father started to complain about. Peter's brother Anthony would not help with the chooks, for any quantity of money that Peter offered him,' well within reason'.

Peter had stopped bringing replacement day old chicks some time ago, and it took a while to slowly sell all the hens and cocks he had, as fresh chickens.

Eventually, there were no more, fresh chickens to eat or sell, nor any eggs.

Ironically, Mrs Harris had said to Peter, that she missed the fresh eggs and chooks.

Bob Bevan, had stopped working at the poultry farm as he had left Gundaroo and had gone truck driving. This made it just too difficult for Peter to continue at the poultry farm, he was quietly pleased about this as it was becoming stale and boring working there.

It was almost the end of 1963, Peter would soon be turning fifteen and had thought about sitting for his school intermediate certificate and becoming an apprentice carpenter, but after speaking with carpenters who often visited the quarry for maintenance or new constructions around the quarry, they told him, that where he lived, out here in the bush, that it would be too hard to get to work for him, as that they worked all over the place, and that he would really need his own transport to make it work.

This was a sad blow, he thought, you just can't win, live in a great environment out here, but it sets you back?

It was a great place to live, Peter thought, he had a motorbike, and an old BSA that one of the quarry workers stopped riding out to the quarry from Canberra as it broke down too much. Peter, with some help from his father, fixed it to a suitable stage for the paddocks. Peter had an old Standard car that, again some one had dumped in the quarry carpark, he and his father also got that going. They had horses to ride, they did take a lot of catching though, and by the time you caught them, you no longer felt like riding them. They had lots of horse gear and saddles given to them from quarry workers who, quite a few, seemed to have an old saddle at home you could have.

All the Harris children seemed to have lots of friends at school, most weekends there would be a friend of one, sometimes two of them staying for the weekend to go horse riding, or motorbike riding and also spot light shooting was a big favourite. Peter's father had upgraded Peter's Stirling .22 single shot to a Lithgow .22 six shot, bolt action repeater. They were on special at Mick Simmons Sports Stores.

It was 1964, Peter had been offered a job as an apprentice jockey with John Edlington, at his stables at the Canberra Racecourse. It meant he would have to live at the Edlington's home in Watson, as part of the conditions for apprentices.

He spoke in some depth about the move with his parents and they seemed to think it was worth a try, as they said, he was pretty good with the horses around the quarry.

Peter continued school until he could complete his school intermediate certificate, then moved into the Edlington home and started work at the stables with Mr Edlington, who said his first job was to stop calling him Mr Edlington, his father is Mr Edlington, but his name is John, call me John!

They started work at four o'clock each morning, by mucking out the stables and getting the horses out and ready for track work. If weather permitted, the horses that weren't having track work were put into day yards. They would then go back to John's home for breakfast at about nine o clock and would not go back to the stables until about two pm, unless there was other work that needed to be done, such as going to John's father's farm at Weetangera, for bales of lucerne hay and other items.

Peter was really enjoying this type of work, with the exception that when, during the day when there was no work until four that afternoon, he was made to read books on horses, or more accurately, (Equus Caballus) a hoofed herbivorous mammal of the family Equine. Peter found most of these books, either boring or hard to read. The books about riding and riding technique, and riding gear, were much more interesting, but John had told Peter that he was not advanced enough for that just now and to get back onto horse maintenance.

Peter's favourite part of the day was early morning and in particular, cantering the horses up to the entrance yard for the course track work. One of John's track work jockeys was named Ted Doon, Peter got on well with Ted, who showed him a better way to hold the reins for more control and how to sit better on the lightweight training saddle.

Peter does not remember what happened, other than saddling Cody 'Coluson', and then riding him down to the yard for track work.

He awoke and did not have a clue to what had happened, he realised he was lying in a bed in hospital, blue curtains were drawn around him, his left leg in plaster and on a pillow, he felt totally bewildered.

He could hear voices from time to time, and he could hear footsteps, but no one came through the curtains and he drifted back into sleep.

He was awoken by somebody calling his name, as he opened his eyes, the left one would not open, a nurse was standing saying "Peter, Peter," and when she saw he was awake, "Your parents are here to see you, Peter, Peter stay wake"

Then the nurse went through the curtain and drew it open at the same time Peter's mother and father walked up to the bed and Peter's mother saying to him "Don't worry love, everything is alright, you've just had an accident but everything is going to be alright"

"I don't know what has happened mum"! Was all Peter could say, as the nurse opened the other two curtains on each side of the bed, allowing his parents to go up beside Peter.

Peter's mother held his hand, asking if he was comfortable, did he need a drink, whilst picking up a small glass of orange juice and removing its little cotton cover and placing a straw into it. Peter thanked her and said he had no idea of what was going on, but the pain in his leg was horrible when he tried to sit up a little to drink the offered juice, he quickly lay back and the pain eased.

Peter's mother, explained the whole incident to him.

I was about seven o'clock this morning, when Peter's father had been loading trucks at his work, when the weigh bridge attendant, June, had walked to where he was and indicated with her hands that he was wanted on the phone. He had finished loading the truck and then driven to the weighbridge, gone inside and picked up the phone. It was John Edlington saying that there had been an accident earlier this morning and that Peter was at the Canberra Hospital, and went on to say that Peter was fine, he had suffered a broken leg and had been unconscious since he fell off the horse he was riding.

Mr and Mrs Harris had driven instantly into Canberra to the hospital, they had arrived about nine o clock and were told that Peter was due to go into surgery at about ten thirty that morning and that they could not see him until about two o'clock that afternoon. But all was well, he is suffering from a concussion and a broken leg, with minor facial injuries.

John Edlington had arrived back at the hospital, as he had to return to the stables to catch the horse. He told the Harris's that he really did not know what had happened, other than that Ted Doon, had ridden up from the course to John looking for the next horse, John told Ted, that Peter had taken it down to him, and then they both realised and started looking.

It was still pitch black at five thirty that morning and Peter, nor the horse could be seen. As it slowly became lighter, they saw the horse in a wheat stubble field, behind the course, but no Peter. As they headed towards the horse, it bolted and jumped a fence into another paddock. It was then that they found Peter face down in the wheat stubble.

John had thought that Peter was dead and as he turned Peter over, Peter let out a sharp cry and then went quiet again. Ted stayed with Peter, as John raced to get his station wagon, neither of them even thought about an ambulance.

Peter was placed into the back of John's station wagon and John headed towards the hospital. He said that Peter regained consciousness a couple of times and screamed in pain on the way in, but was unconscious when he arrived at casualty.

The Harris's, then returned home to see the other children, they had told Anthony and Marilyn, when they were home earlier that morning to just stay there and wait until they arrived home and not to go to school that morning.

They then prepared to return to the hospital at about midday to discover their son had received a broken leg, it had been set and a cast fitted and that Peter was in recovery and that they should be able to see him about three o clock.

Peter spent three weeks in hospital, as his leg had to be reset due to some problem which nobody ever really to found out why?, he did return home however on crutches, but it was four months until Peter could have the cast removed and further two months until he was able to walk unaided by crutches.

During this time, Peter's mother had organised homeschooling to allow Peter to gain the HSC.

During this time of Peter's convalescing, Anthony had left school and joined the Royal Australian Navy, as a junior recruit and was based at HMAS Leeuwin at Fremantle in Western Australia.

Marilyn was still in primary school and had refused to travel to school on the school bus, Mrs Harris had decided to take her to school each day.

The third week of Mrs Harris taking Marilyn to the Lyneham primary, Mrs Harris called into Commonwealth Motors at Lyneham, who were GMH dealers, to get her car serviced. Whilst waiting for the car, she discovered that the dealership was looking for a driveway attendant. Mrs Harris asked the manager if the position hours would work around school hours, which it did, and when she asked if she could apply for the position, the manager, who had seen her buy fuel on a regular basis, as well as her car services, said that if you want the job, it's yours.

This was just perfect for Mrs Harris, as she came in each day to bring Marilyn to school, then again in the afternoon to collect her, she could stay for the day, earn money and save fuel. It was also a plus as the primary school was only two hundred yards from the dealership, which meant Marilyn could sit in the car until it was time for school, and then again after school until her mother finished work.

Mr Harris was not too keen on Mrs Harris's job, but she explained that it was extra money to put away for a house in Canberra one day. Peter thought that Marilyn was spoilt.

As the year turned to 1965, Mrs Harris had decided that life might be easier for both Peter and Marilyn, if the family moved to Canberra.

It would be nice, she had decided, to have her own home, one that was to her selection, not what was available. Mr Harris, who was now the transport manager at the quarry, was no longer required to be on site at all times, and was quite happy to move as it would ease the pressure placed on him by the new loader driver for the house they lived in at the quarry. It would, however, require him to travel about twenty miles each way to work each day.

Every weekend, it seemed to Peter, that Mr and Mrs Harris started house hunting around the Canberra suburbs. Peter joined them on the first two occasions and actually found some really nice homes, but, it seemed that no one other than himself thought the homes were suitable.

CHAPTER 13

Canberra

The homes the Harris's had looked at, either seemed to be too big, too old, too far, or too something or other.

They then discovered a brand new Canberra suburb, currently being developed on the southern side.

Finally, Mrs Harris had found the house she liked, apparently Mr Harris, also thought it was quite good, as they purchased a home at Storey Street, Curtin.

It was quite an easy move from the quarry to Curtin. Mrs Harris did not want to take any of her old furniture from the quarry house as it was impregnated with the dust from the quarry and the dirt road in front of the house, even the fridge.

Marcus Clark's department store, located in the new Monaro Mall in Canberra's Civic Centre, was where Mrs Harris went shopping for most of her new furniture, including curtains and blinds, which they delivered for free.

Peter also enjoyed the new home with his own bedroom that had a window facing the street, he was also pleased to be living in town as it meant better prospects for work.

Mr Harris had mentioned to some of the people working at the quarry, that now they lived in town, it may be easier for Peter to get an apprenticeship as a carpenter and it wasn't long before a maintenance carpenter, called Nils, who was working at the quarry, told Mr Harris about a fellow he know's could be looking for an apprentice, as his former apprentice had finished his time with him, but didn't stay on.

He went on to say that he would most likely see him over the weekend and he would ask.

It was a few days later that Nils gave Mr Harris a piece of paper with the name of Nik Odden and a phone number. He told Mr Harris that Nik could only be contacted on weekends as he worked away during the week, he went on to explain that Nik, a Norwegian, like himself, mainly worked out in the bush on cottages, either construction or renovations, but give him a call to find out.

Peter was handed the phone number of Nik, together with the brief explanation that Mr Harris had received. Peter was pretty keen to talk to Nik and eagerly awaited the coming weekend.

Peter had tried calling the number, just about all day without any success, on the Saturday. He had called the number quite a few times on Saturday night until he just gave it up as a bad joke.

It was on the next day when Mrs Harris asked Peter if he had been in touch with Nik, to which Peter responded that he didn't think the number was connected. Peter's mother said, "Why not give it another go now, I know it's Sunday and all, but give him another try, or you will have to wait until next weekend".

Peter, dialled the number yet again, it rang, and rang, and "Yar, Nik ere" the voice answered.

"Arr, Nik", responded Peter, "my name is Peter Harris.....and...I was given your number by Nils, from the quarry...an.."

"Yar, Nils, from the quarry, you are Peter, yar, you have to tell me the address to get you for tomorrow at six o clock" Nik replied in a very strong accent that Peter could hardly understand. "Do I have the job"? Peter asked excitedly.

"You do want to work or no, it's OK by me, sure, I will pick you up, what is your address".

Peter gave him the address and Nik went on to say, in very broken English, that Peter would need some work clothes for one week, and good boots, they were going out to a property near Araluen, and that it gets ******* cold so bring a jacket.

Peter was awake by four o'clock the next (Monday) morning, ready with his bag packed, mostly by his mother, who had not stopped asking him questions, do you need to take food, where in Araluen will you be, do you need a hat, take a hat, take a thick jumper, wear those thick socks, take five clean shirts and three pairs of jeans, make sure you have breakfast before you go, I'll put some sandwiches in your lunch box to eat on the way, and take your flask with hot tea.

Headlights could be seen coming up Storey Street at around twenty five minutes past six o'clock, as they drew closer, Peter could see it was a Landrover long wheel base ute with a canopy. Peter almost tripped getting out of the house, dragging his bag and his lunch box with him, he went up to the landrover's passenger side and opened the door to find Nik sitting at the wheel looking at him.

"I'm Nik, right to go, hop in we're running late" and clunked it into first gear.

"Where will I put my gear" asked Peter. Nik told him to just push it over the seat and it will be right! Peter tried to settle into the passenger seat, amongst all sorts of items, mainly empty beer bottles.

Nik eased the clutch out and the Landrover lurched forward like it was in a race, Nik apologised and said it was a new clutch, and he wasn't quite used to it yet, and said "I'm Nik, by the way, you want to be a carpenter eh, a chippy a, well its good but you will have to build up a lot, very hard work and it will knock you out if you are not strong.

Nik continued driving and took a drink from the bottle of beer he held in his right hand, which Peter had not noticed. Peter didn't really know what to think, but he thought the worst thing, would be to say anything in respect to the beer.

During the ninety mile journey out to Araluen, Nik told Peter, in between drinks from bottles of beer, that the job they were going to, was a shearers quarters that had burnt down last year, well most of it had burnt down. Nik told Peter that he had been on the job for two weeks now, and had demolished the ruins and that all the new materials required, were now on the site ready for construction.

He also told Peter that today would not be a work day, as by the time they got there, unloaded and set up camp in the mess house, the day would be gone.

They stopped at Braidwood and Nik went into the butcher shop and Peter followed, Nik asked him if he ate steak, Peter, said he had not had it much at home, only mutton, which he was fed up with. Nik told Peter that mutton was shit, as he ordered eight pieces of rump steak and eight pieces of porterhouse steak and four pounds of beef sausages, the thick ones, he said to the butcher as he pointed.

Down two doors to the small supermarket for three loaves of bread, a tub of margarine and a carton of Marlborough twenties, he looked at Peter and asked if he needed some drinks and gestured to help himself. Peter got two bottles of GI cordial. Back to the Landrover to put the food into Nik's giant esky, then back to the shop for two blocks of ice, which Nik placed into another esky.

Then it was down to the Albion Cafe for breakfast. Peter was starting to think that this was going to be quite good.

They continued on to Araluen.

They arrived at the property around eleven o'clock, after what seemed to Peter to be a drawn out trip, trying to understand what Nik was saying to him and bring to count the number of beer bottles that Nik had drunk on the way.

It was a great looking property, just past Araluen in the Araluen Valley. It had a

very impressive entrance, with a 'Y' junction about a half mile in from the gate, as Nik followed the road to the left, there were road grids in place of gates, which Peter also liked as he did not have to keep getting out to open gates.

After about two miles from the entrance, they arrived at the sheep yards, with the shearing shed a little further along the road, then behind the shed stood the cook house and behind that the quarters site.

Nik got out of the Landrover, carrying his bottle of beer, walked to the cook house door. He turned the knob and went inside, Peter followed him and took it all in. It was a fairly large building, they had entered into the dining side which had two very large tables and at least twenty chairs, one of the tables had been moved into a corner and had chairs piled on top of it, and in its place, two metal framed beds with white and black striped mattresses on each bed.

The other table was placed in the centre of the floor, in front of the fireplace. There were four chairs near the table, facing the fire. That was all that was in this room other than a door leading into the kitchen.

The kitchen had a large table in the centre of the room. To one side was a meat hanging and butchering room, similar to what they had at the quarry, but this one was much larger. The other side of the kitchen was a walk-in pantry with shelves of stuff on each side, with another door inside the pantry that led to the store room. A very large, double cook range, with ovens on each side and double fire boxes, this backed on to the fireplace in the dining area, This huge, cast iron stove had a name on the front, 'The Younger'.

Cast iron skillets were hanging inside the alcove of the huge hotplates, on each side. The whole place looked as though the cook had just stepped out for a minute, with tea towels hanging over a chair and other items sitting on the table.

The back wall had a back door, and a long work bench with a double, stainless steel sink with a cold tap coming straight through the wall from the outside. Another tap came from the ceiling down next the cold tap, this was hot water from the stove. Peter, finished exploring the kitchen and returned through the door to the dining area to find Nik, fast asleep, or passed out Peter thought, on one of the beds. Peter went and found the amenities block out behind the kitchen and to his amazement found they were flushing toilets, except after he had finished found they flushed only once. He found the two water tanks on a small hill behind the amenities, and turned on the water until the cistern in the toilet he had used, had finished filling, he then turned it off again as he wasn't sure if it should be on or off.

Nik, was still asleep so Peter looked around the area where they would be working tomorrow. He saw all the rough sawn timbers neatly stacked in different sizes, he looked into a big stack of timber that was covered in tar paper, to see it was not rough like the other stuff. There was a pile of fine sand and next to it was another pile of river sand and gravel. There was also a petrol powered mixer.

Peter had spent the afternoon unpacking the Landrover, of what he thought, should be unpacked and had placed it into the dining area. There was an icebox in the kitchen that looked like two blocks of ice would fit in the lift up top, when placed longways towards the back, so he placed the ice blocks in there. He then took all the meat that Nik had bought in Braidwood and placed it into the refrigerator that sat in the corner of the kitchen, next to the meat room. The refrigerator stunk, after it had been turned on for a while, Peter discovered the fridge was a no goer, and he moved the meat into the compartment below the icebox. Nik was still out!

Looking across the paddocks, Peter saw many rabbits and thought that he would see if he was allowed to bring his rifle with him next week. It was getting dark so Peter thought he would cook himself a steak by using a single burner gas stove that he had found whilst unpacking the Landrover, and a skillet from the kitchen, which looked surprisingly clean, he hoped he could get it as clean when he had finished with it. Before cooking, once again tried to wake Nik, to no avail.

Having cooked a steak and thoroughly enjoying it, Peter cleaned up, found some wood and lit a small fire in the huge fireplace, closed the Landrover, and shut the door to the cook house. Peter then rolled out his compact nylon sleeping bag, that his mother had packed, thanks mum, he thought. Peter then fell asleep to the snoring of Nik Odden.

It was dark when Nik shook Peter and said get up and eat your breakfast, Peter had forgotten where he was for a moment, he got out of bed still wearing the clothes from yesterday, he put on his boots and headed off to the amenities behind the kitchen, the lights were on in the amenities and the water had also been turned on. The little water heater near the row of three showers was making a sshhhhhing noise, so Peter went back to get a towel for a shower, Nik saw him and told him to hurry, his breakfast was ready. The shower Peter thought was really good until it ran out of hot water.

Sausages and toast were waiting for Peter and it tasted good.

It was just becoming light when they emerged from the cookhouse to start work, they went to the shearing shed and opened up a padlocked door where Nik was storing tools, they took a maddock, a pick, a square spade and a square mouth shovel and went to the work site.

Nik explained what they were going to do that day.

When the old place burned down, some of the old stumps they burned too, they were only sitting in the dirt, no concrete, no good, today we will dig new stump pads of one foot by one foot by one foot. These we will fill with concrete and then place the steel, three foot stirrups, the ants don't eat these too much, then we check the height with the dumpy, OK let's go!

It was around five thirty when they had finally finished digging the, seventy, holes then filling them with concrete and setting the stirrups.

Peter thought that it would be the end of the work day, they had not stopped for lunch, just a few stops for drinks of luke warm water and GI cordial from the water bag. "OK, said Nik, no more today, let's rest, big day tomorrow.

Peter was exhausted and wanted to go to bed, but Nik was adamant, "NO, NO, shower first then food, then sleep", he said as he stoked the fire in the cooker, that he had lit earlier.

A huge rump steak that looked like it was still bleeding, potatoes cooked without peeling them and some long green beans that had been cleaned and trimmed were awaiting Peter after he had showered. Nik showered and returned to finish dinner, Peter was starving but he did not think he could eat this meal, it did not look good to him, too undercooked,

Nik dished up the dinner in front of the fire, he looked at Peter and said, "Good Luck, now eat. After dinner, Nik got into his bed and said to Peter, "You wash the dishes, I cooked the meal, ok", and in about two minutes he was snoring.

The next day, was a repeat of the first day except they were placing the bearers and the joists.

The following day, another repeat, except they were starting to make up framing.

On the Friday, when Peter woke, it was light, daylight. Peter jumped up to see what was happening, only to find Nik, still sleeping. "Wake Up" shouted Peter.

He had to repeat this a few times until, Nik said, "Not today, it's Friday, we go home soon, now rest."

It was around ten o'clock when, after eating the last of the steak and the two sausages remaining, the Landrover packed, tools locked up, water and power turned off, then they left the site and stopped at the Braidwood Bank of NSW.

Nik, came out of the bank and gave Peter, two Ten Pound Notes, while looking at him sternly and said questionably "OK?"

Peter could not believe it as it was almost double of what the award rate was. Thanks, oh yes, thanks, that's fine mumble Peter.

Nik, leaving Peter in the car went to the Hotel and came back with a carton of Tooths KB Lager and asked Peter if he drove, Peter said yes, but he did not have a license yet, Nik drove Peter back to his house in Curtin whilst drinking his KB bottles. "Monday, six on the dot, see youse then, OK," said Nik, looking quizzingly.

Peter's mother saw Peter's arrival through the kitchen window, that faced the road, she was so anxious to find out how things had gone. He was no sooner in the door and she was upon him, "well, good to see you home, how was it, did you like it, were you warm enough, did you have enough to eat?" hammered Mrs Harris.

The last question caused Peter to remember that he hadn't eaten the sandwiches that his mother had made for him last Sunday night. Too late as his mother was already unpacking his lunch box and clothes bag, looking for dirty washing, then holding up the sandwiches and looking at Peter questionably.

Peter was trying to drink an orange juice his mother had poured him from the fridge, whilst also trying to answer his mother's questions. She finally said, your father will be home soon, then you can tell us all about it. Thank heavens, thought Peter.

Peter was sitting in the lounge room watching television when his dad arrived home, he walked into the lounge with a bottle of beer and two glasses, "How'd you go matey" his father said, whilst holding the bottle in the air, "want a beer".

That was a first for Peter, his dad offering him a beer. Peter had quite often helped himself to his father's beer back at the quarry, in the shearing shed where Mr Harris seemed to have a very large supply of cartons of twenty six ounce bottles hidden in the wool bale box, and heaps in the sheep chemical's fridge.

Peter, guessed that the currency for the sheep, his father sold, was in cartons of beer.

Peter, and his friends, on occasion, would take bottles from the fridge and replace them with bottles from the bale box.

Peter, was really enjoying his beer with his father and his mother came in to join them as Peter told them all about his first week as an apprentice carpenter.

Peter, stopped talking and looked at his parents, both looked utterly shocked at the whole proceedings from the last five days. Especially the amount of money he had been paid. But Peter assured them that he really enjoyed it and he had learnt so much as this man Nik seemed to know everything.

Peter's father asked if Nik had taken out the tax from his pay, had Peter filled in a tax form, when was Peter going to see the apprenticeship board, where did Nik Odden live, what was the name of the business. Peter, could not answer one of these questions.

Peter's father, told him that he needed to find out these things before too long, and his mother said she would prepare a list of questions for Peter to ask Nik.

Peter's mother did notice that Peter seemed to sleep most of the weekend.

Monday morning, Peter was up and ready to go and had packed his rifle this time, his mother had not made any sandwiches for him, as he had assured her Nik was feeding him very well. He had with him the list of questions that his mother had prepared. With the help of his father, introspect to, tax, apprenticeship board, workers compensation, Nik's company name, and Nik's address.

Nik, picked up Peter at about six thirty, Peter pushed his bag over the back and carefully placed his rifle in the back also, whilst Nik was enjoying a beer, and then away to Araluen again.

Peter thought it might be easier to ask his mothers questions at this stage of the journey before Nik had too many beers. "Nik, Mum wants to know about the tax on my pay"

"Yar" Nik replied, "I pay the tax, tell her no worry"

"She said I should fill in a tax form"

"Yar, I fix, tell her no worries"

"She wants to know, when will we see the apprenticeship board"

"Yar, no rush, finish this job up here first, another few months, tell no worry"

"Do you have, Worker's Compensation, she also asked me, to ask"

"Sure, yar, of course, you need this, it's all good, too much questions, what else?"

"What is your business name and where do live"

"Odden Construction, staying at the hostel on the hill, but I am building a house in Lyons suburb soon, I have a block there now, Olympus Way, we will build after Araluen, you will see, is that all?"

Well, Peter thought, Nik, seemed to have all the answers, everything must be good. No Worries!

On Friday, whilst heading home, after nearly three months, the shearer's quarters were almost finished, just doing the internal fit with Scotia trims, quad and half rounds.

They had stopped as usual at Braidwood, and Nik, coming from the bank, had paid Peter an extra forty pounds, a total of sixty pounds. He then told Peter that he would not need him next week and that he would ring him soon.

Peter felt a bit shocked and upset, Nik must have seen this on Peter's expression and had said, "Nothing to worry about, just take a break, I will get Olympus Way organised, I will call you, you have pay and not to worry, I will call"

Peter never did hear back from Nik, the Carpenter at the quarry, Nils, had told Mr Harris, that he had heard from other friends of his that Nik, had returned to Norway, but that he did not really know.

Peter, this time approached the ACT Apprenticeship Board seeking an apprenticeship as a carpenter. After about two months, the Apprenticeship board contacted Peter with a contact for a possible apprenticeship.

The carpenter's name was Hermann Doric, Peter went to his workshop in Fyshwick for an interview with Mr Doric.

Public transport was also impossible at Fyshwick, so Peter's mother took him for his appointment at the prescribed time of three o'clock, only to discover that the premises were closed. How disappointing, another Nik Odden, Peter's mother uttered as she reversed out of the parking area in front of the building.

Before Peter's mother could drive away, a Volkswagen Combi van pulled up and an oldish, bald headed man jumped out and waved at them to stop.

He came up to the driver's window and asked "Are you Peter?"

Mrs Harris responded yes, he is here, indicating to Peter.

"I am so sorry, my daughter had to leave early", I am Hermann, he explained. "Please come in, I will just park this, and open the door, he said, pointing at the Volkswagen.

Peter started work with Mr Doric, who was not only a carpenter but also a locksmith.

Doric's work was very diversified and inculed, home building and renovations, new home fit outs, and some metal fabrication, including security bars and screens.

Doric also had a contract with a company that supplied fire rated doors for home units, and installation of these complete with lock and door closer.

Peter enjoyed this work and attended the Reid TAFE every Tuesday as an apprentice carpenter.

In 1966, on the 14th of February, decimal currency finally came in, a little late for Peter, but still it helped him.

Then the following year 1967, Peter was conscripted to the Australian Army, but as he had an active apprenticeship, was deferred to serve for three years in the CMF.

And thus ended the first ten years of Peter's new life in Australia.

Although it may have seemed to have been a great adventure, which it was in many ways, However, Peter, his brother, and sister. schools lives suffered in many ways, due to the constant moving to different schools, never settling into a school may have resulted in a much poorer education in theory, however, in Peter's instance, it may have produced a better education, in practice.

Peter, went on to marry and have two sons, that reside in the Australian Capital Territory, they have wives and family and have never known more than one town to live in. Such a stark comparison to their father.

They have never been told this part of their father's life.

The end?

not really, as there has been much more to Peter's life since he left the ACT in 1989, but……..that's another story.

www.ingramcontent.com/pod-product-compliance
Lightning Source LLC
Chambersburg PA
CBHW072059290426
44110CB00014B/1749